D0008962

The book, *Eyes to See*, flows out of God's grace through a family already committed to life giving ministry. The stories of growing faith during their dark struggles while watching their young son Jesse lose his vision are heart breaking. We can discover with Becky and Tim the perfect gift of God's grace. As Tim says, "God's grace and the fulfillment of faith in His promise will amaze us, beautify us and fortify us with grace and healing."

Dr. Robert and Kay Bickert
Veteran missionaries to the Philippines

I first met Tim and Becky Keep while they were serving in the Philippines. In my observation, the challenges of rearing a child who is blind have made them better—stronger, more compassionate, and more effective in ministry. You will be deeply moved and challenged by their story.

Randy Weisser
Director, Resources for the Blind, Manila, Philippines

There are a plethora of books about faith and spiritual victory, but few match the transparency and candid story of *Eyes to See*. In the pages of this book, you will discover the honest openness of simple faith when faith is not simple. With this heart-wrenching story of a father and mother who walk with their little boy as he steps into blindness, you will find confidence for your journey.

Rev. Blake E. Jones
Pastor, Christian Leader

As you read *Eyes to See*, perhaps like me, you will find yourself laughing at the funny moments, or weeping over the heartbreaking loss of sight to such an innocent child. More importantly, as you finish the last chapter, I hope you will say as I did, "What a faithful, all knowing God we serve, who allows us to see glimpses of Himself and His goodness in the midst of pain and suffering."

As a sister to Becky, I've had the privilege to watch close up their strong confidence in a God who holds all of our tomorrows safely in his hand. While their journey has not been one without hardship … it has also not been without our loving God there to rescue them when they felt as if they couldn't go on another day … Never once through the good, bad, and even ugly times of their story, have I witnessed Tim or Becky's faith in a sovereign God to waiver. Tough times, oh yes! Heart breaking moments … too many to count! But, if you had the opportunity to ask Tim and Becky, "Were you ever forsaken by God?" you would hear them confidently answer, "Never!"

Kim Collingsworth
Sister, Concert Artist with The Collingsworth Family

I'm thrilled that Tim and Becky Keep are writing their story. Not only will those four years be accurately recorded for their children and family, but sharing in book form the details of God's faithfulness will be a blessing to many others! What an act of vulnerability and trust for them to share their innermost hearts with us!

Cathy Parker
Pastor's wife, Friend

EYES to SEE

GLIMPSES OF GOD IN THE DARK

EYES to SEE

GLIMPSES OF GOD IN THE DARK

BECKY KEEP
with TIM KEEP

Contents

———◀✍▶———

Contents

ACKNOWLEDGMENTS

Words could never adequately express my thanks …

- To the many friends and supporters who stood by us, expressed their care in countless ways, and prayed us through the tough days.

- To our awesome family who laughed with us, cried with us, and never failed to show up when we needed them most.

- To Valerie and Timothy Jr. who, though young, bravely endured the sometimes difficult task of being the siblings of a cancer patient. I adore you both!

- To Carolyn and Samantha, who have filled our lives with joy and also given Jesse a run for his money and … someone to pick on!

- To our national leaders and Christian friends in the Philippines who encouraged us by their own remarkable stories of God's grace, and by their patient endurance through many trials and afflictions.

- To Ann Sheehan and the wonderful staff and friends at Shoreline Pediatrics who stood with us through every bump in the road.

- To Dr. John Roarty, Dr. Jeff Taube, and so many wonderful nurses and friends at Children's Hospital of Michigan. You are much more than medical professionals … you are good, kind and caring people.

- To Rev. Blake Jones and Rev. Larry Smith, and my dear friend, Christina Black, for reading the manuscript and offering such thoughtful advice and encouragement.

- To Brandon Hilligoss for sharing his incredible design talents and creativity with us.

- To Tim who loved, supported, and bolstered my courage to write this account. Thanks for your hours of creative input and for seeing this project through.

- To our wise, powerful and good Heavenly Father whose love never fails. It is our *deepest* desire that your excellent greatness will be illuminated to all who read this story.

FOREWORD

WHY ARE STORIES TOLD AND RETOLD? What is the value of a story? Why was Jesus' ministry marked by parables and common interest narratives? I think stories are conveyors of truth in a way that nothing else can match. Narratives open the shutters of our minds to light and beauty that otherwise would remain hidden to our view. Somehow, real-life accounts with their emotional tug and identifiable, common feelings allow truth to step into the light, statements to morph from drab facts to brilliant realities, and concepts to take on substance.

Tim and Becky Keep have a story to tell. You will enter their emotional darkness as you follow the progression of Jesse's cancer. Becky will take you to the moment as you sense her heart freeze with terror on her roller coaster-ride of trauma. The helpless ache that filled the hearts of us who surrounded the Keep family will become yours as Jesse descends into earthly darkness. But, was it a descent into darkness or an ascent into light—God's light? The Scriptures declare that, *"The way of the righteous is like the first gleam of dawn, which shines ever brighter until the full light of day"* (Proverbs 4:18 NLT).

The story that calls to you from the pages that follow will give trust in a good God a new and tangible beauty. If, for you, faith is forever just out of reach, Becky will share the story of her heart until,

I believe, you will be able to embrace the God of the Bible into your own story. Nothing of the human experience and taunting doubts will be sugar coated. This is not a book of lofty platitudes but of faith struggling to see God's face in the darkness. You will laugh at Jesse's wit; you will cry with his mother, and you will yearn to put your arm around his daddy's shoulders. But, when you are finished, you will find that this account has given you a fresh grip on faith.

To the glory of the God of Heaven and His tender healing, the trauma of Jesse's blindness has not defined the Keep's existence. They are not draped in the pervading blackness of Jesse's sight-less world. Instead, they radiate the simple but elegant strength of one who has faced the darkness and now lives in comfortable surrender and happy relationship to the good God who is fully trustworthy—the God of Light.

Now, as has already been the case for many others, you will find yourself telling and retelling parts of this story to your family and friends. It will bear repeating time and time again as you seek to drive back the suffocating darkness and make Light visible to others grappling with questions that they cannot answer.

It is my prayer that as you read these pages, the first rays of heaven's Light that have warmed and beckoned your soul will rise into a blaze of glorious reality and joy.

Rev. Blake E. Jones

INTRODUCTION

ON A BEAUTIFUL SUNDAY MORNING IN 2005, Timothy and Jesse, our two sons and I found ourselves in a small, wooden native house-church in the poor village of Caritas. We were high in the Cordillera mountainous region of the Philippines. Surrounded by tribal people who had recently come to saving faith, we joyfully anticipated this morning of worship with them. They seemed ready to blend their hearts and voices in praise to the one who had set them free. Our weariness from the steep and rugged jeep ride and considerable hike the day before had given way to eager anticipation as well. As far as I'm concerned there's no better place to be on a Sunday morning than worshiping Jesus with those whose love for Him is simple, sincere and fervent!

The villagers of Caritas seemed eager, and a bit curious, to meet Jesse. They knew something of his story. They knew that he was totally blind and that this blindness had come at the end of a long battle with cancer of the eyes. I knew some of them had prayed *earnestly* for his healing, and I wondered if they felt perhaps that God had let them down.

As we all worshiped together that morning I'll never forget the gentle moving of God's Spirit among us and the sense I had that He wanted to do something special for us. I don't know what particular sufferings may have been represented by the Caritas believers gathered that morning, but I do know that life for most of them is hard. I do know that more often than not their favorite Scriptures and spiritual songs carry themes of trial and affliction and God's faithfulness to carry His children through. I do know that living testimonies which magnify the grace of God *in the midst* of sorrow and grief often speak to them in ways nothing else can. Just before the message was to be delivered, "Pastora" Alice talked a little about Jesse's story and requested that he play a song on his king flute, an instrument he was just learning to play. Timothy accompanied him on the guitar. I'll never forget the song they selected:

> *Amazing Grace, how sweet the sound,*
> *That saved a wretch like me.*
> *I once was lost but now am found,*
> *Was blind, but now I see.*
>
> *'Twas Grace that taught my heart to fear.*
> *And Grace, my fears relieved.*
> *How precious did that Grace appear*
> *The hour I first believed.*
>
> *Through many dangers, toils and snares*
> *I have already come;*
> *'Tis Grace that brought me safe thus far*
> *And Grace will lead me home.*
>
> *The Lord has promised good to me.*
> *His Word my hope secures.*
> *He will my shield and portion be,*
> *As long as life endures.*
>
> *When we've been there ten thousand years,*
> *Bright shining as the sun.*
> *We've no less days to sing God's praise*
> *Than when we've first begun.* ~John Newton

The beautiful and yet haunting tones of the flute and guitar filled the house and lifted our hearts heavenward. Though I have rarely seen tribal people show strong emotion, as our nine- and twelve-year-old boys played, almost every eye brimmed with tears. Some wept softly. Some bowed their heads in silent prayer. The Lord's presence was so real, and even after the music ended we sat basking in that presence while wave after wave of healing grace poured over our little congregation. Minutes passed and still no one spoke. It seemed to me that the music and the lyrics and a young boy's experience of heart healing all blended together to form a complete testimony of grace. It was a story which underlined the truth that what Satan intends for evil in our lives, God sovereignly works for good. When Alice finally found her voice she did not magnify Jesse, but rather the *faithfulness* of God to all who love and trust Him, the very thing my wife Becky longs to do through the simple telling of this story.

We live in a fallen and yet beautiful world. As I travel to other countries of the world I notice that every culture has its own unique flavor, that the peoples of the world are wonderfully diverse and colorful, and I enjoy this uniqueness immensely. While countries and cultures differ in so many ways, they each have this in common: they are filled with suffering people! Since this is true—since the experience of suffering is a common experience—when one learns that a fellow sufferer has found grace in suffering, he takes courage in his own. Grace is contagious! Comfort begets comfort! A wounded healer is a trustworthy spokesman for the grace of God. Becky and I are humbled by how the Lord continues to use our *limited* experience with suffering to inspire hope and healing in other lives.

Life is hard! No matter how "successfully" prosperity-gospel preachers are selling their deceptive version of "faith" around the world, it is still hard. While in one particular Asian country last year, I especially saw the devastating aftermath of prosperity-gospel preaching. So many sincere believers all over that vast country, teeming with souls, have been taught that faith is defined, not as child-like trust in God as Father, but as a weapon Christians use to batter a reluctant God into compliance with their will, that faith not only has the right to demand what it wants but *will* receive what it has demanded. And yet ... believers in that land, and in every land, continue to experience profound suffering.

Let's face it! Prayers sometimes go unanswered; loved ones suddenly pass away leaving us with unspeakable grief; painful thorns are often left to preserve in us a broken and contrite heart; business ventures sometimes fail; children sometimes wound us ... deeply; friends often disappoint us. Faith just doesn't *guarantee* miraculous results, promise immediate justice or alleviate all suffering. What good is faith then? Faith does promise that God will show up! Faith does promise that grief is never ultimately wasted. Faith *does* promise that God will redeem every moment of pain for our good and His glory! Faith does promise that faithful suffering through "light affliction" which is only for a moment, *"is working for us a far more exceeding and eternal weight of glory"* (2 Corinthians 4:17). Faith *does* promise that God will amaze us, beautify us, and fortify our faith with glimpses of Him even in life's darkest valleys. Faith *does* promise that in His time God will mend and heal our heart! This is our testimony.

I'll never forget a particular moment just a few months before Jesse's sight would suddenly be taken from him. It was a crisp, clear and starry Sunday evening, and I was trying to push my family out the door so we wouldn't be late for church. Timothy and Valerie ran outside and jumped in the van while I moved Jesse in that direction just as fast as his little legs would motor. He hurried to the open door but then stopped quite abruptly on the threshold, threw his curly head back and cast his gaze heavenward, taking in the brilliant night sky! After a few moments I heard him exclaim with breathless, child-like wonder in his voice, "Hey Dad! Look at the stars!" We did not know it at the time, of course, but this was one of the last glimpses of the stars he would have while living on this earth.

Becky and I believe that each of us needs to pause once in a while and take in the splendor and majesty of God, especially when we suffer. Looking up has transforming power. By looking up we discover grace and healing, for as the Scripture says, *"Every good gift and every perfect gift is from above, and comes down from the Father of lights, with whom there is no variation or shadow of turning"* (James 1:17). As you read our testimony I think you will agree with me that the Lord has helped Becky lift our eyes to the all-sufficient One, the all-gracious One, yes, the One so willing and able to help us in our time of suffering. Her prayer and mine is that the Lord will use something in these "glimpses of God" to comfort you, strengthen you and fortify your faith for the journey ahead.

Tim Keep

CHAPTER ONE

Blindsided!

"For you created my inmost being;
you knit me together in my mother's womb
My frame was not hidden from you
when I was made in the secret place
When I was woven together in the depths of the earth
Your eyes saw my unformed body
All the days ordained for me were written in your book."
Psalm 139

OUR LIVES WERE ABOUT TO BE CHANGED FOREVER!

Tim and I cringed as the doctor placed tiny metal clamps on both the upper and lower eyelids of our five-week-old son, Jesse. His piercing screams broke our hearts, and had it not been necessary to hold his small squirming body on my lap, I would have covered my ears to drown out the painful wails he emitted during the ordeal. It was six o'clock in the evening on October 30, 1997, eleven days before we were scheduled to return to the Philippines where we served as missionaries.

EYES TO SEE

We had awakened hours earlier to what promised to be a lovely autumn day in central Michigan. The air was fresh and cool and the sun was shining. We were staying at the home of my parents in Edmore, and were on the last leg of our four week stay in the USA. These final few days would be spent resting at Mom and Dad's—especially restful for me as I had just given birth five weeks earlier. Nothing can quite compare to being at "grandmas" with a new baby. I was relaxed and enjoying the extra help with our two older children, Valerie seven, and Tim Jr., three.

Knowing that we were serving in the center of God's will had made it no easier for me being so far from my parents during the previous year, our first year of service in the Philippines. I am the sixth child born into a family of nine children and had been raised in a ministry family with Dad either pastoring, working in evangelism, or being involved in Bible college administration as long as I could remember. We children had grown up traveling the country with our parents—all nine of us, packed into an old station wagon. It was often amusing to see other passing motorists trying to count how many of us there were as we sailed down the highway, en route to our next place of ministry. We'd usually just hold up nine fingers to save them the trouble! Dad would preach revivals and camp meetings; Mom would play the piano and we'd all sing. I don't know how my mother kept her sanity, but we made wonderful memories and have always been close. Each of us children knew that our parents had relinquished us to God at an early age, and we were reminded of this often while growing up. Even so, it hadn't been easy for them—watching us load their two small grandchildren onto a plane and flying more than ten thousand miles away.

Valerie and Timothy were so excited to be spending the beautiful day with Grandma, Grandpa and cousins. There would be Hide and Seek in the fragrant grove of pine trees behind the house and maybe a ride on Grandpa's tractor. Tim and I were looking forward to this day also—a well-baby checkup for Jesse, a lunch date eating yummy, American food and maybe a stop at the mall.

Jesse had been delivered in the Philippines by a wonderful doctor in the city of Manila. Although I had suffered no small amount of worry over giving birth in the third world, it had actually turned out to be a great experience. We had received some of the best care the country had to offer; nevertheless, I wanted him to be examined by our own state side medical professional as well. Once we returned to the Philippines, getting to a doctor we trusted would entail a long and exhausting trip from our home in the province to the capital city of Manila. I just wanted to be sure, so we made the hour long drive to the doctor's office.

Tim and I enjoyed visiting with our friends there at the office and showing off our handsome new son. It was great to see our friend Ann, a pediatric Nurse Practitioner who had taken care of our children for several years before we began overseas ministry. I had even worked for her periodically when one of the full-time nurses was on vacation or sick. She and I had developed a close friendship, and she was absolutely wonderful with the kids—the kind of person who you knew "loved her job." After a thorough exam she stated, "You have a beautiful healthy baby."

Reaching for our jackets and preparing to leave her office, I paused, suddenly remembering something that my mother had expressed a few days before. "Becky, I think something might be wrong with Jesse's eyes," she had said as she slowly waved her hand back and forth in front of his face. "He doesn't seem to follow very well."

To be honest we hadn't taken Mom's fear very seriously. I reminded her that it had been a long time since she had mothered a newborn, but I guess I underestimated the fact that Jesse was her twenty-fifth grandchild! Mom was very "into" her grandkids and had even come all the way to the Philippines to be there when Jesse was born, which is saying a lot, as Mom never has been one to enjoy overseas travel. I guess we thought she was being overly protective, but just to be on the safe side I paused and somewhat laughingly said, "Hey by the way, Ann, would you check Jesse's eyes before we leave? My mom thinks he's blind! You know how grandmas are!"

Ann pleasantly picked up her ophthalmoscope and shined the light into Jesse's eyes. We watched her hesitate and then repeat the process a few more times. "Hmm, you're not going to believe this, but there does seem to be some kind of abnormality in his left eye," she said as she replaced the instrument. "I don't want you guys to worry too much because it may not be serious at all, but I do want this to be looked at by a specialist right away. I'll set up an appointment for this afternoon." Ann's secretary made arrangements for Jesse to be seen by a very reputable pediatric ophthalmologist in Grand Rapids.

Neither Tim nor I felt overly concerned as we made the 45 minute drive to his office. We had no premonitions of the painful turn our lives were about to take. Surely this would be a quick in and out appointment, and whatever this problem was would be cleared up soon. What could possibly go wrong on such a beautiful autumn day in America?! We turned east on I-96, and I popped in a new Christmas CD—a Gaither Homecoming Christmas, hot off the press! Life was good. God was good.

After hours of waiting in a small examination room, we began to get a little impatient. Patients came and went, and we wondered why we were being pushed to the bottom of the list. Several of the doctor's assistants and at least one intern had examined Jesse throughout the afternoon, but they were careful not to betray their alarm. And we couldn't understand why he hadn't shown up. I remember thinking it curious that so many different people had looked into Jesse's eyes, but still we had been given no indication as to what might be wrong. "The doctor will see you soon," they reassured us, as the hours ticked by. And then finally, after all other patients had been seen for the day and the only family left in the office was ours, he stepped in the room.

I felt a flicker of trepidation when he shook our hands, and his first words were, "Hi, my name is Dr. Droste, and I'm very concerned about your son." He apologized for our long wait but assured us that his delay was in order that he might spend as much unhurried time with us as might be necessary.

While Tim and I fought to keep Jesse still, he shone a bright light into Jesse's dilated pupil, and a machine magnified the inner recesses of his retina. Everything the doctor was seeing was also showing up on a screen next to us. We watched the screen, and although I had no clue what I was looking at, in an effort to shake the uneasiness that I felt I said, "So, this is what a cataract looks like?" Dr. Droste straightened up, looked kindly yet soberly into our faces, and spoke the following words that sent a tremor of fear running up my spine. "I'm sorry to have to tell you this, but this is much more serious than a cataract. What I'm going to tell you now" he continued, "is the worst news that you'll ever hear about your child."

Tim and I sat in stunned silence as this specialist explained to us that he was nearly one-hundred percent sure that our son had "Retinoblastoma," a rare cancer that affects children under the age of five. He said that Jesse had a large malignant tumor in his left eye—that the cancer may have already spread to his brain. I felt confused and devastated. How could a newborn have cancer? I wondered aloud. Had I done something wrong during my pregnancy to cause this? How is this going to affect Jesse's life … our lives? Is Jesse going to die?

Dr. Droste told us to forget about going back to the Philippines. He informed us that this was going to entail a very long and arduous course of treatment. When we left his office, it was long past closing time. All but the waiting room lights were turned off, and only a couple of people were left in the office to receive our payment. Walking out the door and down the hall, we were suddenly called back by Dr. Droste. He joined us in the hallway, gave me a quick embrace and spoke very comfortingly, "Don't worry, we've caught this early … and most importantly, you have God on your side!" We had God on our side! I'm sure neither Tim nor I could have imagined how prophetic these words were on that night and how much we were going to need God during the next four years.

And so began our journey into the long, dark and sometimes silent tunnel of the unknown. On this journey the Lord would teach us many things about Himself that I'm sure we could never have learned any other way. Along the way we would taste bewilderment, fear, pain, the drudgery of waiting, days of mind bending questions, and ultimately the unthinkable reality of blindness. We would taste none of these in their raw form, however, for each taste of sorrow was seasoned with generous amounts of grace.

The treasures we would uncover along God's chosen path were to become too priceless to calculate: the peace of God that defied reason; His everlasting arms that slipped underneath us just as we were free-falling through our chasm of suffering; the Spirit's insights which illuminated our hearts in moments of near despair; and the comfort of God's presence even when He chose not to say the things we wished He would say or do the things that we so longed for Him to do. These are just a few of the wonders we would discover. We would learn that suffering for the Christian is never meaningless and without hope for *"... we also glory in our sufferings, because we know that suffering produces perseverance; perseverance, character; and character, hope"* (Romans 5:3-4).

CHAPTER TWO

——◆◆◆——

The Comfort of God's Sovereignty

"It is when we are in the way of duty that we face giants;
when the Israelites turned back to the wilderness, they found none."
Streams in the Desert

"If I had not felt certain that every additional trial
was ordered by infinite love and mercy,
I could not have survived my accumulated sufferings."
Adoniram Judson

WE HAD RESERVED THIS BEAUTIFUL SUMMER DAY OF AUGUST
1996 as a day for rest and recreation. What an incredibly busy year
it had been. In early spring, after much prayer, we had answered
the unmistakably clear call of God to serve as missionaries in
the Philippine Islands, a land neither Tim nor I had ever set foot
on. I was twenty-five and Tim was twenty-seven. In May we had
resigned from the pastorate of a small congregation in western
Michigan. Also in May we had sold nearly every earthly posses-

sion we owned (which wasn't much), paid off a few small debts and positioned ourselves for a whole new life overseas. In June we embarked on this exciting … and terrifying missionary voyage by traveling thousands of miles to many of our denomination's churches, scattered from Michigan to Alabama, and sharing the vision and calling God had given us. By August our two children, Valerie, five, and Timothy Jr., two, had memorized nearly every word of *Send the Light* and *Rescue the Perishing* as well as Mommy's and Daddy's "boring" missionary talks, and these poor little people were getting kind of restless. In fact, we all were!

Our departure date was set for October 17, only a few weeks away, but on this late summer day we had no obligations. We decided that the best way to spend this rare day off was to be with family in the Indianapolis area. Later in the day, my sister Kim and I secured a babysitter to stay with all our children for the evening, and of course, they were ecstatic about spending this time with cousins. Tim and I, along with Kim, her husband Phil, and another of my sisters, Julia, along with her husband (also Tim's brother) Dave, made plans for supper out and a late evening stroll around beautiful Union Station and the downtown area. We had no premonitions that this would be anything more than a simple, relaxing evening with people we loved.

After a nice supper we drove downtown, parked near the city's circle and perused the shops, taking in the sights and sounds of the city and enjoying the warm summer air. At around ten-thirty in the evening, we ducked into a twenty-four hour restaurant for a milkshake, and at about eleven we decided we'd better head for home and rescue our babysitter!

We left the shop, climbed in the van and headed up the street. As we did so, we noticed an unusual commotion up ahead—a group of ten to fifteen white males shouting obscenities at passing cars, cat-calling women and well, making a lot of noise! The closer we got to them the more clear it seemed to us that they had had a little too much to drink. Tim and Phil were sitting in the front seats and rolled down their windows for a better look. As we approached the intersection where these men were crossing, our light turned red. While waiting, we watched a sad drama unfold in front of us.

On the other side of the intersection and facing our direction sat a young black male in a convertible, top down and radio blaring! While we continued waiting for the light to change, the men on the sidewalk stopped, looked at him, shouted some epithets and gestured as if to challenge him to a fight. The black male shouted back, but we couldn't make out what he said, and just as tempers were reaching a boiling point our light turned green. As we moved slowly through the intersection and past the shouting parties suddenly the men on the sidewalk rushed into the street and swarmed around the convertible. "Turn around! Turn around!" Tim yelled to Phil, who was driving, "Those guys are going to beat up that black man!"

We quickly alerted a mounted police officer, who happened to be sitting on her horse near our turn around, and headed back to the scene of the struggle. Tim jumped out of the van and worked his way through the traffic and the crowd already gathered at the scene. He was puzzled at first when he saw that the black man was in handcuffs, thrown up against his car, and some of the men we had just seen on the street had their guns trained on him! We later learned that they were off-duty police officers who had just come from a downtown bar.

Being a very just man, my husband became more and more angry. "What's going on here!" he shouted to one of these officers. "I saw what happened … I saw you guys antagonize this black man …

Who are you anyway? I saw what happened!" "You didn't see anything," the man threatened. He reeked with alcohol.

We remained at the scene until a lieutenant arrived, and Tim, along with dozens of other witnesses, could offer their version of this terrible injustice which had just taken place. The lieutenant was very interested in my husband's account and included it in his police report.

The following days were a blur of reporters, phone calls from the prosecuting attorney's office, an interview conducted by two Indianapolis detectives, and a grand jury testimony. This was a pretty big deal! Not only did this street brawl have racial overtones but there were police involved, and one city official who was running for higher office was pressured to resign. And the newspapers seemed to like the fact that the "star witness" of this case was a minister.

When all the fury died down, Tim was told that if he would agree to a deposition we would be free to continue with our plans to go to the Philippines as scheduled. They would no longer need him as a physical witness. We were relieved to put this behind us, and we left as scheduled to begin our missionary work in the country of the Philippines.

It was early September of the following year that we once again received a phone call from the District Attorney's office, requesting that my husband fly back to Indianapolis to testify in person. They could not subpoena him, but they really wanted him in the courtroom on October 13th. Honestly, I had nearly forgotten about the ordeal. Our lives had been a whirlwind of adjusting to a new way of life, a new country, a new people and culture. That incident seemed a lifetime removed from the life we were now living. Furthermore, my mind was consumed with the impending birth of our third child who was scheduled to make his grand entrance on the 24th of September.

Tim regretfully told the staff member that he wouldn't even consider leaving me and our two older children alone in a strange country and that he could not come. The phone call ended, and we assumed that that was the end of the whole matter.

A few weeks later, as I lay recovering at St. Luke's Hospital in Manila, having just given birth to Jesse Alexander on the previous day, the phone rang next to my bed. I was surprised to hear the voice of the District Attorney. "Please tell your husband that if he will agree to testify for us in this trial, we will buy tickets for your whole family." He volunteered to call the airline to see how soon my baby could fly. Tim and I discussed it, and although I couldn't bear to think of an 18 hour flight with a six and three year old, plus a newborn, we decided that Tim would perform his civil duty. We would pack up and go if we could get Jesse's birth certificate and passport in the very small window of time that we would have.

The hospital was a five-hour, rough and bumpy ride from our home in the province. I was to be released on Friday morning, and we planned to try to get all the paperwork done that day as making an extra trip back to Manila before flying out would have been quite physically difficult for me. In our last conversation with the Attorney we had told him that getting all the paperwork done in such a short amount of time in the Philippines was a really long shot, but that we'd give it a try. Those who have ever tried to get official work done in a hurry in the developing world will realize just how long the shot really was. Only later did we realize just how powerfully God was working for us.

From the time we checked out of the hospital at around noon, things began to fall into place with amazingly little effort on our part. The birth certificate was secured at Quezon City Hall in only minutes. (Having now birthed two additional children in the Philippines we realize just how "miraculous" this was.) In a small Kodak shop we propped our two-day old little guy up long enough for them to get a passport photo and waited forty-five minutes for the prints. Would we make it to the Embassy by the three o'clock deadline? We knew it would be close.

Back on the street we hailed a taxi and headed for the US Embassy. I sank into the soft seat already exhausted and weak, not only from childbirth, but from the oppressive September heat! Traffic was surprisingly light for a Friday afternoon in Manila, and we arrived at the US embassy much sooner than expected but only fifteen minutes before their windows closed for the weekend.

While we waited for Jesse's passport to be processed, a missionary walked over to me and with a smile said that she and her husband were having an argument over how old our baby was. "He looks like a newborn but he can't be!" she exclaimed. "We noticed that you're getting his passport today, and we've been trying for over a month to get one for our newborn but only today have been able to get it!" "What's this all about, Lord?" we wondered.

We could not possibly have understood the significance of the day's events or the events which had taken place over the past year. Our loving Father was shoving mountains aside for us, but His movements were taking place beyond our horizon. There was so much going on that we just couldn't see.

After leaving the embassy, we stopped at Jet Travel to purchase tickets for our flight to Indianapolis on October 10, and then had a peaceful dinner at one of our favorite American restaurants—a fitting celebration of the success of the day and especially the birth of this newest member of our family. Mission accomplished!

THE COMFORT OF GOD'S SOVEREIGNTY

Now here we were, five short weeks later on October 30, 1997, buckling our son into a car seat that was as new as he was, and doing so with hearts of lead. There was no joy, no celebration, and although we hadn't eaten for hours, the mere thought of food sickened us. What was going on? A cancer diagnosis wasn't in the plan! We were missionaries! We had heard God's call and were obeying that call! Why had we been given this beautiful child—a gift from God, only to be told that there was a deadly disease lurking in his eye? That we might lose him, and that we now had no home, no work, no ministry, no certainties concerning the future, was absolutely breathtaking. With those words, "Your son has cancer," our lives had come to a screeching halt. What is God thinking!?

Jesse slept in the backseat, gloriously oblivious to it all, while Tim and I began to talk on that long ride back to my parents' home. Our minds were drawn back to the events of the past year: God's call, our answer, the months of preparation, the crime, the timing of Jesse's birth, the timing of the trial, fast taxi rides through the busy streets of Manila, the unbelievably easy securing of birth certificate and passport, the conversation with the missionaries at the American Embassy. Suddenly, unexpectedly, we were aware of God's powerful, soothing presence in the car with us! It was awesome!

What we felt in those moments was more precious than life itself. We felt peace which passes understanding! We felt divine love! We even felt joy! Darkness fled in the light of His presence. In those moments the sun shone gloriously through broken clouds of fear and confusion, and we began to get a very clear look at the face of our heavenly Father. We felt loved and cared for as we had never felt it before. He had known and prepared for this moment long before Jesse was even conceived! Unbelievable! Immeasurable comfort! Overwhelming grace! God's strong, steady hand was in control. Moments of thick blackness would sometimes seem to envelop us in the coming days, but at this moment we had no doubt that this present crisis had not taken Him by surprise.

Tim and I suddenly understood that although our world was rocked to the very core, this cancer diagnosis was not in control, and most certainly, Satan was not in control. Our minds were overwhelmed with the truth that our Heavenly Father was in control. He had a plan. He had intended this for His glory, and He was ordering our steps. He knew what He was doing, and He was looking out for us and, most certainly, for our little baby.

As Tim and I traveled through picturesque farm lands toward my parents' home, we actually began to praise God as we rejoiced in His sovereign care. He had a plan and we could rest in that plan. His presence and peace flooded our hearts as we realized that if two sparrows cannot fall to the ground without our Father's knowledge, then surely He knew intimately about us. His participating presence had already been at work in our lives, preparing us for this great trial that He knew was coming.

The knowledge of God's sovereignty and presence was a defining moment for us and a reference point that we would refer back to time and time again over the next four years.

We were emotionally drained by the time that we arrived back at my parent's house. They knew nothing of the news that we had just been given. The house was full of people and was bustling with activity. My sister Sandy and her husband Melvin and their six children, (missionaries to Ukraine home on furlough), were also staying there.

I remember thinking, "How do we even begin this conversation?" The reality of it all washed over me in a torrent as we began to spill out the details of our day! To hear my own voice saying the words, "Jesse has cancer!" was surreal. We tried to protect our older children from the grave nature of this, but Valerie, always perceptive and a very "old" seven year old, cut right to the chase! "Is Jesse going to die?" With those words, I was assaulted by a fresh wave of fear and uncertainty as I realized that I couldn't answer her. I honestly didn't know what was going to happen to my son!

As quickly as possible all eight children were tucked into bed for the night. I smelled the aroma of fresh coffee and realized that Dad had made a fresh pot. There had never been a time in my life when Dad had not brought comfort and perspective to my fears. I was thankful that he and Mom were here. We adults settled down in a small sitting room just adjacent to the kitchen. We talked in muted tones so as not to waken the kids and went over everything that the doctor had said, racking our brains and trying to remember every detail. The warmth of family wrapped itself around Tim and me like a cozy blanket; we were calmed and comforted just feeling their love and support. Dad led us in prayer, and we all committed Jesse to God. Afterwards Tim and I fell into bed exhausted in every way.

My sleep was short-lived as Jesse didn't know that he was "sick" and wasn't about to skip his midnight meal. As soon as I heard him stir, I was awake and eager to spend some time with him. The house was dark and still as I carried him to the rocking chair in the sitting room. I nursed him and held him for a long time. I kissed the top of his head, closing my eyes and savoring the sweet smell of him. I opened the blanket and took in every perfect detail of this sweet child of mine, from his tiny fingers and toes, to his dimpled knees, and the soft wrinkly skin around his ankles. He was beautiful! I looked into his dark eyes and tried to detect what the doctor had told us was there. I saw nothing. I wondered how it could be that such a perfect baby could have something so sinister threatening his life. He looked no different than he had 24 hours before, and somewhere deep inside of me was the hope that this was all a dreadful mistake that would be cleared up with the dawn of a new day.

We found ourselves at Children's Hospital of Michigan the very next afternoon. Someone in a white coat came out and put drops into Jesse's eyes to dilate them. We then waited … waited … and waited. I watched people come and go for hours. I saw kids with crossed eyes, patched eyes, swollen eyes, and even the tiniest tots sporting thick lens glasses. I wondered what their stories were.

Finally we were called back to see Dr. John Roarty. He was younger than I expected but put us at ease immediately with his warm smile and kind, professional manner. Tim sat in a chair holding Jesse while Dr. Roarty, wearing a strap around his head with what looked like a miner's light beaming from his forehead, examined Jesse's eyes. He used the light and also what appeared to be a small round magnifying glass. After what seemed like an eternity, he sat up and confirmed to us what we had been told the previous day. Tim and I were full of questions.

He told us that Retinoblastoma is a cancer that occurs in babies and small children under the age of five. We learned that it happens in about 1/100,000 live births and that it is a genetic form of cancer that can be passed from generation to generation. He also told us that if untreated this disease is 100% fatal, but with modern medical intervention 96% of children will survive. He went on to say that this wasn't going to be quick and easy but rather a long ordeal. We must be patient, he said, and hold on for what he described would be a roller coaster experience, meaning that our hopes would be raised, dashed, raised and dashed again. How right he was! He described perfectly what we were about to experience in the months and years to come.

THE COMFORT OF GOD'S SOVEREIGNTY

We left that day on information overload. It was Friday and we were to return on the next Tuesday when Jesse was scheduled to begin his chemotherapy. We had yet to meet with the Oncologist, but we had had enough for one day.

And so began our journey into the world of the sick! We became weekly patrons of Children's Hospital, and the Ronald McDonald House became our second home. I won't soon forget our first night there. We were assigned a room and shown around the facility. It was beautiful with all the amenities that one could possibly need. There were many other families there, and I wondered what had brought them to this place. It was overwhelming. As we were getting settled into our room, I placed Jesse on our bed and walked across the hall to the bathroom. Moments later I returned and was shocked to find a very white, very bald, and very naked three-year-old boy up on my bed leaning over Jesse's seat and talking to him. He turned to look at me, and I inhaled sharply when I saw a long thin tube protruding from the middle of his chest. (I later learned that this was how he received his chemotherapy.) I gathered my wits about me and asked this weirdly cute young man what his name was. Before he could reply, a wild eyed and screaming woman came running around the corner and into my room. She was red-faced and crying. She frantically grabbed my newfound, naked friend and barely introduced herself before exiting.

This was the beginning of what would be a four-year friendship of sorts with Donna and Tyler. We would be recruited to help search for this little guy as he would often "hide" from his mom, even going outside and running down the street without his clothes on! I learned that living with a sick child can bring out the best and sometimes the worst in people's emotions, and on several occasions over the next few years we prayed with this single mom when she felt that she could not endure another day.

On this same evening, another very well-meaning mom asked me why we were there? I explained that Jesse was starting treatment the next day and would have a central line inserted. With a knowing look and a smile she called her little boy over and proceeded to pull his shirt up, showing me what we were in for. For her, it was as common as if she were sharing a favorite recipe! She meant well, but I was horrified and had to excuse myself. I went to my room, held my tiny baby in my arms and cried. I wanted to run away! We didn't belong in this world of tubes, baldness and funny looking contraptions placed under the skin.

In that moment, I lost sight of the overall big picture of God's sovereignty that had seemed so real only a few nights earlier. We were now entering the trenches of the nitty-gritty details of what this cancer was going to require of us—what Jesse was going to have to endure, the ugliness and invasiveness of this diagnosis and the reality that this was going to alter our "normal" forever. Everything in my being wanted to reject this situation. I didn't want to accept this as being something that was under the control of a sovereign and loving God. This wasn't supposed to happen to us—to our son.

Later as Tim and I prayed together in our room, we began to see that we had to keep what we knew about God right in the forefront of our hearts and minds. It wasn't going to be easy to see Him in the messiness of all the details. We couldn't be carried on some lofty emotional feeling that "God is sovereign." The reality of this situation crashed into our consciousness with blunt force, and our emotions were tenuous and untrustworthy. We would have to place our faith and feet firmly on what the Word of God says about who He is. This knowledge would be the only foundation for our faith and strength during the long days of waiting, uncertainty, and yes, sometimes fear that we would experience. This was no time to run, but this was time to face the future with the knowledge that we were not alone.

CHAPTER THREE

———◄✍►———

God Really Is Good

"Oh, taste and see that the LORD is good;
blessed is the man who trusts in Him!"
Psalm 34:8

THE BIBLE IS FULL OF VERSES DECLARING THE GOODNESS OF GOD. In John 10:11 Jesus declares, *"I am the good shepherd."* The Psalmist invites us to, *"taste and see that the Lord is good"* (34:8). Again, in Psalm 119:68 we read, *"You are good and do good."* Because God's nature is good, His works are good too.

It's not difficult for Christians to acknowledge God's goodness while their circumstances are pleasant, their health good, their marriage strong and their children thriving. But this is not always so when we find ourselves in situations which scream for deliverance.

Why is it that we sometimes equate God's goodness with the absence of personal pain? Is not suffering God's good gift to us too?

Isn't it through pain that He reveals Himself in ways He could not in life's joyful moments? And how will we ever prove the power of His Word except to test it in life's most challenging moments? *"Underneath us are the everlasting arms"* is a promise of God's infallible Word, but we'll never feel the comfort of those arms until we are made to release our last thread of hope and free-fall into them. H. C. Trumbull said, "Blessed is sorrow for it reveals God's comfort."

It gradually dawned on us that Jesse's illness was not going to be of the swift and brutal order, but rather the long, drawn out and often excruciatingly, monotonous order, and that the key to survival would be to hold out hands of faith for daily portions of grace. And at every turn God gave us glimpses of His goodness.

Our new "normal" in the days following Jesse's diagnosis would become the pattern of our lives for the next four years. Every few weeks we would leave our home at four-thirty a.m. and drive the three and a half hours to Children's Hospital in Detroit. Jesse's chemotherapy infusion would begin at eight o'clock a.m. under the supervision of Dr. Jeff Taube and would take approximately three hours. He would then be taken to the Operating Room where Dr. Roarty would perform an EUA (examination under anesthesia) and apply laser treatments directly to the tumor. The combination of the chemo and laser was known to be quite effective in destroying these tumors.

These were very difficult days. Jesse couldn't eat or drink anything from four a.m. until after his surgery was completed. Having to deprive my newborn of his regular feedings for 8-10 hours was heartbreaking. While he would scream, refusing to be consoled, Tim and I would take turns walking with him as we pulled along his IV pole. Occasionally, out of sheer exhaustion, he would fall into a fitful sleep, and we'd all have a few moments of reprieve.

By the time Jesse was taken back for laser treatment, Tim and I were most often worn out, hungry, and I was usually a little nauseated due to the underlying anxiety I felt. We would sometimes take turns sneaking down to the cafeteria to quickly grab a cup of coffee and a donut. I would sit there, letting the coffee and sugar work their magic, but all the while feeling guilty thinking of my hungry little guy upstairs.

After the EUA and laser treatment the doctor would meet with us in the waiting area, (where many other anxious parents waited too), and tell us how the cancer tumors were responding. Finally, after an hour in the Recovery Room we would get to take our hungry, worn out and irritable baby home. A follow-up EUA was always required a week later in order for the doctors to further evaluate the results of the treatment. After two weeks the whole process would begin all over again. And so it went for nearly forty-eight months.

After Jesse's diagnosis we faced the dilemma of where we would live. We obviously couldn't live with my parents indefinitely, and going back to the Philippines was out of the question. The very week that Jesse was diagnosed, the church we had pastored prior to becoming missionaries suddenly lost their pastor due to some severe physical problems. They had heard of our situation and asked Tim if he would consider coming back as pastor once again, at least on an interim basis. After praying about it we felt clearly that this was the leadership of the Lord. We moved into the parsonage almost immediately, and these wonderful people filled the parsonage with furniture, towels, dishes and everything that we could possibly need.

It's easy for Tim and me to see, now, how ministry responsibility at this time was a gift from a good God. Having a place to serve the needs of others, while struggling with needs of our own, yielded the fruit of spiritual and emotional health. Service made us accountable, kept us spiritually fit, and helped to ward off the lethal viruses of self-pity and introspection. God was good, and He knew that service would turn us outward and be a means of grace in our lives.

As we entered the troubled world of cancer and met dozens of families dealing with long-term, life-altering disease, we noticed that too often they allowed the battle to define their very existence. Because of this disease focus their most important relationships, left untended, began to suffocate from the weeds of conflict and misunderstanding. Though it took quite some time, the Lord graciously taught my husband and me that our lives would be defined by what we chose to fix our gaze upon. If we would choose to make cancer our focus then cancer would define us, and everything in our peripheral vision—God, each other, our children and others—would die from neglect. People might say, "Oh look, there goes that poor family dealing with cancer, and just look at how it has wrecked their lives!" But if we made God our focus then our lives would be defined by Him and His good purpose, and He would receive the glory! People would say, "Oh look, there goes the people whom God is helping, His grace preserving, His Word purifying, His love nurturing, His presence beautifying and His power sustaining in the furnace of affliction! What an awesome God they serve!"

My husband and I have slowly come to understand that God is glorified when His children refuse to be defined by crises—a disease, an accident, an injustice, a divorce or any other life altering experience—but rather by God Himself.

GOD REALLY IS GOOD

I mentioned earlier that the doctor warned us to "hang on tight" as this cancer journey would often give the feeling of being on a terrifying roller coaster. How right he was! Jesse's cancer was so unpredictable. One week we'd get a great report—"All tumors look dead!"—only to come back two weeks later and hear Dr. Roarty refer to the tumors as "disturbing" or "worrisome." Those words would reverberate around in my head for a week as I wondered what in the world was going on in those little hazel brown eyes, and the next week we would often learn that the cancer was growing again.

The bad reports terrified me, but the good ones taunted me—as if to say, "Things are looking up today, but don't get too comfortable because the stomach-sinking drop is lurking just around the corner." I grew to dread these visits and would start feeling anxious a couple of days before each EUA. More often than not I would spend the night before Jesse's appointment tossing, turning and watching the clock. After each examination I would anxiously study the doctor's face as he walked through those steel doors toward us, trying my best to prepare for what he would say. It was emotionally draining to say the least.

An excerpt from my journal dated March 12, 1998, is one example among many of the breathtaking disappointments we often experienced:

> "Our worst fears confirmed today. Dr. Roarty found a tumor in Jesse's right eye and several more in his left. I am so shocked! I don't really think that we expected this. I was so optimistic this time … my poor baby!"

45

EYES TO SEE

One day when Jesse was almost two years old, we took him for his regular chemotherapy treatment which was to be followed by laser surgery. After the nurse hooked him up to his infusion, we took him and his siblings to the toy room to play. He was starving as usual and a bit grumpy. Suddenly he began coughing excessively and then to struggle for breath. I quickly grabbed the first nurse that I could find in the clinic, and she immediately shoved us into a room and called an emergency. Jesse was having a severe reaction to the chemotherapy!

Medical personnel immediately stopped the infusion of chemotherapy and began giving IV drugs to counteract the reaction. Jesse's surgery was immediately canceled as there was no way any anesthesiologist would intubate him in this condition. We had to stay for several more hours for observation, and by two o'clock in the afternoon he was beside himself with frustration and hunger.

As we prepared to leave the office Jesse noticed that his sister, Valerie, was eating a piece of candy. He begged and pleaded for a piece, and out of pity I told Valerie to go ahead and let him have one. Jesse immediately began to choke because the candy had lodged in his throat, and then he turned blue! I tried desperately to dislodge the candy, and so did Tim and the nurses, but without success. Tim held Jesse while I ran frantically (and rather impulsively, I think) down the hall and burst into a conference room where a number of doctors were in the middle of a meeting. As soon as they heard my plea for help they jumped out of their chairs, sending them flying backwards, and ran to assist! As I raced back to Jesse's room, I heard someone call a code blue over the loud speaker and realized that they were calling it for him! I couldn't believe it!

Just about the time everyone poured into the room, Jesse coughed up the candy and began to breathe again! We were shaken to the core. Tim felt as weak as a kitten; I was crying; the nurses were crying, and I remember one nurse telling me, "Please take this baby home to a safe place. We've almost killed him twice today."

Minutes later two exhausted parents and their children turned out of the hospital parking garage and headed for home. We rolled along for a while trying to unwind, sometimes caught up in thoughts of how differently things might have turned out today. But we were still together. Jesse was safe. What else could go wrong? Then it happened! Somewhere between Detroit and Lansing, on what seemed like the loneliest stretch of highway in the state, the engine sputtered … and died! Tim knew what had happened even before he turned onto the berm and coasted us to a stop. He let out a little groan and looked at me incredulously. "I forgot to get gas!" he said flatly.

It was absolutely too much for one day, and to be honest, this wasn't my finest moment as an understanding wife! It was my first, and I trust, my last hitchhiking experience. We must have looked pretty pitiful that blazing hot afternoon—this family of five standing hot, hungry and disheveled beside the highway trying to hitch a ride! But God was merciful and sent a "Good Samaritan" along to take us (all of us) in his car to the next gas station and then back again.

Hours later, after tucking the children into bed, Tim and I sat in our living room feeling too drained to speak, but too grateful to complain. How merciful God had been today. We were overwhelmed with a sense of peace and gratitude for God's goodness. How certainly we would have stumbled today had not our heavenly Father carried us. It had indeed been a day like no other, but every frightening detail only accentuated the fingerprints of God's love and care for us. We were home. We were safe. Our love for one another had survived and possibly even grown stronger. We were in this thing together, and our three children were sleeping peacefully. We served a good God, and we were not alone in this battle!

EYES TO SEE

Shortly after Jesse's adverse reaction to the chemotherapy occurred we were back for yet another exam. This time Dr. Roarty regretfully told us that because Jesse's body was now resisting the chemotherapy it was no longer an option for him. He said that we had lost our "Big guns" with which to fight this cancer and would have to resort to using other smaller weapons now.

A few months earlier we had tried another treatment in addition to the chemotherapy. This one, also known to be very effective, was a radioactive plaque sewn directly onto the surface of the tumor. A lead lined patch was then placed over the eye to protect Jesse and everyone else from exposure, and he was placed in isolation for five days. On the fifth day the plaque was removed, and the results were evaluated. In the beginning this treatment seemed to work well, and within a couple of weeks the tumors looked totally dead. We were thrilled. But by August, the most worrisome tumor was back with a vengeance. We were running out of treatment options fast.

In November, 1999, Dr. Roarty pressed us to make a decision regarding Jesse's left eye. He really felt that the tumor was viable, even pressing on the optic nerve, and explained that if this tumor were to break through the wall of the nerve it would have a direct pathway to the brain. This terrifying prospect made the decision to allow the left eye to be taken a fairly, simple one. The question was, will it be an eye or a life? It was not an easy decision for sure, but there was never really any dilemma involved in making it. Jesse would still have one healthy eye, and we felt pretty confident that the Lord would preserve it that way.

On November 18, 1999, Tim donned a surgical gown and mask and carried our two-year-old little guy into the OR, holding him tight until the anesthesia carried him into a deep sleep. It was a very emotional day for us, for on the one hand, we were saddened to have lost the battle with this eye, but we were also relieved that the worst part of this cancer—the part which threatened his sight and his life—was gone for good! Or so we believed.

We were very weary too. The thousands of miles traveled, the endless days of waiting in oncology clinics and waiting rooms, and the relentless treatments were wearing us down. Tim and I really wanted to put this nightmare behind us and move forward with life. We wanted Jesse to know a life outside of hospitals and operating rooms. On this day we were told that the right eye was in great shape. There were tumors but they were minimal and appeared to be dead. We were hopeful that this would be the beginning of the end of the matter.

Two days after the removal of Jesse's left eye we returned to Dr. Roarty for the removal of the bandage. We had been instructed to "leave it alone," and this was fine by me for the mere thought of seeing what lay beneath that bandage sickened me. As Dr. Roarty began peeling away the bandage he admonished us to prepare for a shock. Nothing could have prepared us, however, for the sight of our little guy. His face was black and blue from the trauma of the enucleation. There was an ugly hole where there had once been a beautiful hazel brown eye. I felt weak and sick to my stomach. "Help me Lord!" I breathed, while fighting the urge to bolt from the room. Somehow He held me together through the checkup, but on the ride home I cried, thinking of how this surgery had so disfigured my beautiful baby. I didn't want to walk this road. This was way too hard.

Later that evening, Tim and I were startled by both screaming and laughing in the hallway of our home. Upon investigation, we found Jesse, very much aware of his newly found status as the "one-eyed kid" in the family, chasing his siblings through the house declaring himself "A Monster!" While Timothy and Valerie acted frightened they were also laughing hysterically! We laughed too, of course, and it was probably about the best medicine we could have taken that night; a welcomed blessing from a really good God.

I learned personally that night that Christians in crisis often find that joy pushes through sorrow and triumphs over it much like a tender green shoot pushes through black soil and rejoices in the glory of the springtime sun. What a miracle of grace!

I was anxious for Jesse to be fitted with an artificial eye as soon as possible. He refused to leave the patch on, and he looked a little like an abused child without it. I couldn't even take him to Wal-Mart without him being subjected to curious stares. We were told that after a few weeks we could get a temporary prosthetic eye; one that wouldn't necessarily be custom made but would work until the socket was sufficiently healed and a permanent mold could be poured.

As we traveled back to Detroit to meet with an ocularist, I felt a little inward trepidation. The whole idea was a little scary to both Tim and me, but we were anticipating Jesse's having a normal looking eye again and were interested to see just how this process would play out.

The day of the fitting we were met by a no-nonsense, though not unkind, older gentleman who sported a quiet, nonplussed approach to the whole proceeding. We would learn in the days to come that the skill of prosthetic eye-making was acquired primarily through years of apprenticeship, that it required an artistic gift few possessed (especially in the painting) and that Dr. Terry had distinguished himself as one of the top ocularists in the nation. We would also learn, however, that being a good ocularist doesn't make one a warm, skilled communicator.

He introduced himself quickly and got down to business. We received no gentle explanation about what was going to happen, nor were we asked if we had any questions or concerns. Rather without warning, Dr. Terry instructed Tim to hold onto Jesse, and when he was satisfied that Jesse couldn't move he pried open the socket for a quick look. I watched aghast as he then swiveled his chair around and opened a drawer full of prosthetic eyes of various sizes and colors. I shuddered inwardly as I heard them clattering around like marbles in a tin can as his deft fingers searched for just the right one. He finally found it, held it up for a better look, and then took Jesse from Tim's arms, put him in a firm headlock and quickly popped it in.

I must admit that right about then my protective motherly instincts were rising as quickly as my blood pressure! This man was making me angry! I think I interpreted his silence and directness as rudeness and his firmness as meanness. Why wasn't he explaining every action? Couldn't he talk us through this? Couldn't he be a little gentler? I mean, we're not buying a pair of shoes here! This is an artificial body part!

The only way to deal with this was to trust this … stranger. Jesse was yelling in protest, and I was about to! A moment later, however, Jesse stopped screaming, his head popped up, and when he looked at me, I saw, not a vacant empty hole, but a beautiful brown eye. My anger dissipated immediately, and I went from wanting to hurt Dr. Terry to wanting to hug his neck. He had taken our son's disfigurement and in a moment transformed him back into a normal looking little boy. I could have cried for joy!

I learned a great lesson that day about how we sometimes view God in the midst of our suffering. In my impatience I have wanted answers and explanations all along the way, but He has been silent. I have felt angry when God hasn't met my expectations, and there have been times when I have tried, unsuccessfully of course, to press Him into a stereotype of my own creation. I have often failed to realize that just as Dr. Terry's expert knowledge and experience promised a beautiful outcome, so God's skilled craftsmanship of our lives promises a magnificent, glorious end as well. He does not obligate Himself to inform us of His often mysterious movements though, but He is glorified as we learn to trust His wisdom implicitly.

I am learning that because God is good, I can rest in the knowledge that I will ultimately find all His ways to be good as well. The longer I live and the more grace I experience, the more assured I am that we serve a good God; One who delights not in pain, but in the giving of, *"beauty for ashes, the oil of joy for mourning, the garment of praise for the spirit of heaviness"* (Isaiah 61:3). My life, Jesse's life, and your life is defined by Him and His good purpose.

CHAPTER FOUR

———◆◆◆———

A Walk of Faith

*"True faith drops its letter in the post office box and lets it go.
Distrust holds on to a corner of it
and wonders why the answer never comes."*
Streams in the Desert

"Never be afraid to trust an unknown future to a known God."
Corrie Ten Boom

IN EARLY 2000, as the cold, harsh western Michigan winter began in earnest, our hearts were warmed and encouraged by the steady flow of positive reports from Jesse's doctors. We were encouraged and believed that Jesse's cancer was gone for good.

During an appointment at Children's Hospital on February 3, 2000, we received an "All tumors are dead" report. Dr. Roarty felt that given Jesse's age, (he was two and a half years old now) and the usual course of this cancer, he was probably "out of the woods." Tim and I gratefully leaned into the hope that perhaps there was a light at the end of this tunnel. We tentatively brought up the subject of our returning to the Philippines and were surprised at

Dr. Roarty's optimistic response. He believed that it was safe to resume our plans to return and even approved our tentative date of late October. We knew, of course, that we must continue having checkups every three weeks or so until that time. We also planned to find a doctor in the Philippines who would do follow up exams, just to be sure. One of Dr. Roarty's colleagues had a trip planned to Manila the following year and consented to see Jesse at that time. We were told that most children have no reoccurrence of this cancer after the age of three and almost none after the age of five.

Tim read his resignation letter on a cold Sunday morning in late February. It was sad, for we loved our congregation, but we were so excited to be returning to what we knew that God had called us to. It was so hard to believe that this ordeal was actually almost over! We were elated and began making preparations for our return. Tim had continued to give leadership to the expanding Filipino mission work even while pastoring and caring for our family during the time of Jesse's illness. Our congregation had been very patient with the six strategic trips he had made to the Philippines over the last two years. Now he was anxious to get back to this thriving ministry on a full time basis.

Our Mission board asked us to travel to our supporting churches during the summer of 2000. They desired that we would raise the necessary funds to build a new mission house. I was thrilled to be given this project. The house that we had lived in before was made out of wood and literally eaten up with termites. I recalled my shock at having fallen right through the kitchen floor while eight-months pregnant with Jesse. I knew that I had gained weight but not that much!

My journal entry for March 27, 2000, reads,

> *"Time is flying by, we received yet another fabulous report*

on Jesse from Dr. Roarty. Thank the Lord! Our plans are full speed ahead for returning to the Philippines in October."

It was an exciting time. Jesse was full of fun and vigor and kept us laughing. He was becoming very interested in his "fake eye." Valerie was horrified one day when he walked up to her and said "Look sissy!" She glanced down to see that he was holding out his hand with his eye sitting right in the middle of his palm!

One Sunday morning while talking with some visitors in the vestibule just before the service began, I looked down at the floor and was jolted by Jesse's eye staring up at me. He had decided to take it out and throw it down. I kept talking, calmly bent down and scooped it up before our guests noticed what it was. When his Grandma Keep called to talk with him one day, he said to her, "Guess what, Grandma, my eye came out." He then threw his head back and gave a great big belly laugh!

And then there was the day when Tim looked up from his studying to see Jesse standing in front of his desk with a very noticeably missing left eye and both hands thrust deep into his pockets. "Jesse, where is your eye?" Tim calmly asked. "It's in my pocket, Dad," he matter-of-factly replied!

I've heard horror stories of children actually taking their "eyes" out and swallowing them. Thankfully, we never experienced that!

The spring of 2000 was a fun time. All of us began to relax a bit as life seemed to be easing up. We were granted a Make-a-Wish trip for Jesse in April and enjoyed a wonderful and relaxing week in Florida. A limousine ride, a beautiful suite at the Boardwalk Hotel and tickets to all the Disney parks in Orlando was a dream vacation for us all. The long, early, morning drives to Detroit and the smell of hospitals seemed a lifetime away as we played the days away. It was a joy to watch not only Jesse, but especially Valerie and Timothy Jr. having such a good time. Late in the evening, we'd watch college students perform magic shows on the boardwalk while we ate rich and sugary elephant ears. The kids got to meet all their favorite Disney characters as well. Before returning home, we spent another week visiting both our parents who lived in Florida at the time. What awesome memories we made!

We took Jesse back to Detroit for an appointment on the 18th of May. It had been a busy week as we were preparing for a yard sale to sell all the things that we had accumulated during our time in the US. I had advertised this sale in the newspaper and planned to get rid of everything down to the forks, spoons, and bath towels. My sister, Sandy, had come to watch the kids and planned to stay the weekend to help us with our sale.

Dr. Roarty came out to talk to us after the exam. His words were startling! "Things aren't good," he began solemnly. My heart slammed into my ribs as he told us that the tumor closest to the area of Jesse's central vision was definitely growing again and would need more treatment. "This is treatable," he said, in an attempt to be optimistic. He laid out the next course of treatment which included "Cryotherapy" which he explained in laymen's terms as simply freezing the tumor. "This is often effective in destroying the RB cancer cells," He explained.

We walked out of that hospital and into the sunshine with hearts and limbs of lead. Tim and I were absolutely numb with the news that we had just been given, and we just couldn't seem to process it. What in the world was going on! Were we at yet another crossroad? I had just recently read in *"A Path through Suffering,"* written by Elisabeth Elliot, that "God is always and forever for us." Why then, had He allowed this? We had prayed much about this decision and had felt God's definite leadership to go back to the Philippines. Had we missed it? This and numerous other unanswerable questions were swirling through our minds. I was in turmoil just thinking of my son, but also of my home where everything that I owned was stamped with a price tag, waiting to be sold tomorrow! What were we to do? Tim called our mission leader, Gary Brugger, who was also our dear friend and mentor, and one who had stood with us during every step of this journey. Tim simply asked him to please pray for us. He then said he needed to rest and asked me to drive awhile. He reclined the seat and fell asleep, leaving me alone with my anxious thoughts.

An hour later, Tim sat up and said with conviction in his voice, "Becky, I know what we are supposed to do. If I have ever heard the voice of God I've heard Him just now!" I listened as he shared that as he was awakening from sleep his thoughts immediately flew to our dilemma and that he began to silently plead for the Lord's wisdom. Suddenly his thoughts drifted to a biblical phrase from Hebrews 11:8, which reads: *"By faith Abraham obeyed when he was called to go out to the place which he would receive as an inheritance. And he went out, not knowing where he was going."* That phrase, *"And he went out, not knowing where he was going,"* began to resonate powerfully in my husband's heart and he knew that the Lord had answered his prayer almost as quickly as he had prayed it. Tim said simply, "Honey, I believe … I'm sure that the Lord is asking us to step out in faith; to stay on course; to trust Him with the future we cannot see …" Though we didn't realize it then, this was to become a defining moment in our lives.

I had learned to trust my husband, and honestly, making decisions was way too much work for me at this juncture. I was happy to leave that to him. As Tim spoke I felt a peaceful confirmation in my heart and heard God also saying to me, "Trust Me."

On May 20, 2000, I wrote in my journal,

> *"We had a great sale and the Lord helped us to get rid of almost everything. I am so tired and this place is a wreck! We went to Sis. Shafer's for supper tonight. Every time I think about Jesse I get a pain in my heart."*

On the 28th of May we had our final service with our congregation. It was a lovely Sunday morning, and we closed out our ministry with a pitch-in dinner and baptismal service. Tim was blessed to baptize one of our neighbors whom he had led to the Lord during her struggle with cancer. What a beautiful time, and she has since gone to be with the Lord.

We had a full slate of missionary services scheduled for the summer of 2000. We needed to raise $40,000.00 to build the new mission home in the Philippines. My sister Julia and her husband Dave were pastoring a church in Concord, Michigan, and offered to allow us to use their home as our base. They had two extra bedrooms, a bath and a family room in their basement. All this became ours for the summer. Although we were rarely there, it was great to have a place to go when we did have the occasional few days free. And my sister Julia was medicine for me! After tucking our children into bed at night, and with our husbands standing guard, we'd sometimes head to Denny's where we'd eat, relax and laugh! It felt so good to laugh!

Jesse had the Cryotherapy treatment on the 25th of May, and when we returned on the 31st for a check-up, we heard, "So far, so good." We were cautiously relieved! A part of me, however, was afraid to trust this bit of good news. I trusted the doctor's expertise, but Jesse seemed to defy all their statistics. Every treatment that we were told was successful 96% of the time never worked on him. He always seemed to fall into the 4% range. This was a constant source of anxiety for me. I had to constantly remind my heart to keep its hopes in the Lord and His purpose.

We lived a rather nomadic life during the summer of 2000—traveling from church to church—sharing our vision for the Philippines. The five of us traversed many Midwest and Southern states, sandwiching quick trips back to Children's Hospital in Detroit for Jesse's checkups. Many times I was tempted to question God's wisdom in leading us to what humanly seemed absurd. I wasn't oblivious either to the questioning looks in the eyes of some who simply could not understand why we were doing what we were doing. Honestly, there were numerous nights when even I felt ludicrous standing up in front of congregations of wonderful people—people who were giving their money to build us a new mission home—when I scarcely had the faith to believe that we'd ever get back to the Philippines. I wrote in my journal that summer:

> "Humanly speaking, we're crazy. It's uncanny though how we both feel like God is going to do something strong for Jesse. We feel no leading to stop our plans for the Philippines, but to continue on taking one small step of faith at a time."

It was during this time that I discovered this beautiful hymn that ministered to my heart:

> Jesus I am resting, resting
> In the joy of what Thou Art;
> I am finding out the greatness
> Of Thy loving heart.
>
> Thou hast bid me gaze upon Thee,
> And Thy beauty fills my soul,
> For by Thy transforming power
> Thou hast made me whole.
>
> Simply trusting Thee, Lord Jesus,
> I behold Thee as Thou art,

EYES TO SEE

And Thy love, so pure, so changeless,
Satisfies my heart;

Satisfies its deepest longings,
Meets, supplies its every need,
Compasseth me round with blessings;
Thine is love indeed!

Brightness of my Father's glory,
Sunshine of my Father's face,
Keep me ever trusting, resting;
Fill me with Thy grace.

Jean Sophia Pigott

(© *Jean Sophia Pigott, Hymns of Consecration and Faith, 1876*)

These words were greatly comforting to me, for Satan tormented me greatly during the entire summer. I often felt weighed down with stress and anxiety, and it all culminated together in a painful lump in my throat which I lived with for five months. I could barely sing and sometimes talking was difficult. I understand now the toll that stress can take on our bodies. I desperately desired, but did not have, perfect trust. I continued to, by the grace of God, cultivate an obedient heart, and I'm thankful that God understands our humanity.

In spite of the conflicting emotions and hectic schedule that we were keeping, the kids were great sports during the entire summer. They did grow weary of the endless, "boring" missionary services though. One Sunday evening as we pulled into a church parking lot for what would be our third service of the day, Jesse piped up from the back seat in an exasperated voice, "Not again!" And then there was the night when, while I was speaking, Timothy, who was six years old, tuned everything out and proceeded to turn two songbooks into a drum set. He was banging away with perfect rhythm.

All eyes were on him, and I had no one's attention. I finally had to say from the pulpit, "Timothy, could you please put your drums away!" God was so good to us. By the end of the summer, we had raised more than the amount needed for our home. I would write, however, *"I'm sick to death of hearing myself speak, and Tim is boring me to tears."*

We were nearing the end of the summer; our deputation travels were over, and Jesse's eye was not clear. On August 29, 2000, we were told by the doctor that, not only was the tumor bigger, the cancer was also still viable and growing. I wrote, *"My mind knows that God is good, and He still loves us, and that He does have a plan in all of this. The pain is just so great!"*

The disappointment was crushing. The possibility of blindness was once again rearing its ugly head. We knew at this point that there would be no October return to the Philippines. Tim had a speaking engagement down in Florida the first weekend of September, and then he was scheduled to speak for a week in a church out west. After that, we had no idea where we would live or how we would survive. We were both under tremendous duress. What if we had misinterpreted what we felt God had told us to do? Surely others thought that we were foolish. Was God going to come through for us now? Matthew Henry said, "We must depend upon the performance of the promise when all the ways leading up to it are shut up. For all the promises of God in Him are yes and in Him Amen!" We were definitely in a place where all the ways leading up to the promise of our going back to the Philippines seemed to be "shut up." The question now was whether we would be able to depend upon the performance of the promise.

While in Florida, Tim and I were able to take a couple of days to celebrate our twelfth wedding anniversary. We went to an island nearby and enjoyed time together, walking on the beach and trying to relax. We prayed and talked and tried to make sense of it all. We were at a dead end! We were going to Oklahoma where Tim would preach a week-long revival, and after this we were going to be officially homeless! Our children needed to start school. I was in despair, and there are no words that I could write to describe how desperate we were. We had not one open door or even an idea of where we could live. There was no Plan B because we had wholly abandoned ourselves to God's calling. Part of me was tempted to wonder if God was keeping His end of the deal—I correct that, nearly all of me was tempted to wonder this.

After returning to my parents' home to collect our children to go … somewhere, my sister Sandy and her husband Melvin called, and out of the blue, offered to let us stay in a house which they owned in Michigan. They had purchased the house a few years before as a home base for their family, (they were missionaries in Ukraine at the time), but they had been desperately trying to sell it. They needed to sell it! And so the arrangement was made for us to stay in the house until it sold.

A few days later we turned off State Route 46 and onto a bumpy, dirt road. A mile later we parked in front of a cozy, country ranch home which our family has named affectionately, "The Little Yellow House." It was situated on a gently sloping hill at the end of a long drive. There were several acres of field bordered by lovely pine trees and a porch swing which I grew to love. This would not only be our home for sixteen months, it would also be a place of physical and spiritual rest!

The very week that we moved into this house, the lump in my throat disappeared, and a sense of calm and restfulness settled over me. It was the last and most difficult months of Jesse's treatment which culminated in his blindness, but we also view these months as precious gifts from God. The house was a haven to return to after each difficult trip to the hospital. In the evenings, when the weather was warm, we walked the quiet, country roads together, often stopping at a shallow creek to let the kids throw rocks into the gently moving water. On crisp, autumn evenings we built roaring bonfires and played delightful games of hide-and-seek in the dark. One winter day after a heavy snow, the kids built a huge snowman right on the deck where he stood guard for weeks. In all, these were months when we rested in God's care, prayed, played with our children and allowed our heavenly Father to cradle us in His embrace during what was, on some levels, a very dark time in our lives.

We enjoyed the fellowship of a wonderful church family who loved and supported us daily. The pastor of our church and his wife, Blake and Saundy Jones, were an amazing blessing to us. We would often stop by their house to talk after a difficult appointment in Detroit.

And what of the house? Although we had shown it to prospective buyers repeatedly during those months, it did not sell until just weeks before we were scheduled to fly back to the Philippines. As a matter of fact, the closing took place on the very day that we moved out. This was yet another confirmation to Tim and me of God's unfailing love and His watchful care for those who offer Him even imperfect trust and trembling obedience. My sister will also testify to the fact that God miraculously took care of her family's financial needs while they were waiting for the house to sell.

When we finally boarded the plane for the Philippines on February 6, 2002, it was comforting to know that waiting for us in that far off place was a beautiful, newly-finished mission home. It had been built during the final sixteen months of Jesse's treatment. More than this, however, we were returning to a calling—a people and land that we had grown to love. Faith, which had patiently, and ever so gently, beckoned us to follow, albeit over long and winding roads, had led us to this moment. We were full of gratitude that, in spite of our sometimes faltering and hesitant steps, our obedience was being rewarded.

To those who traverse troubled waters, Lettie Cowman offers this powerful reminder: "Jesus Christ is no security against storms, but He is perfect security in storms."

CHAPTER FIVE

———◄✦►———

Praying for a Miracle

*"Miracles are a retelling in small letters of the very same story
which is written across the whole world
in letters too large for some of us to see."*
C. S. Lewis

I'VE NEVER KNOWN A FAMILY FACING LIFE-THREATENING ILL-
NESS WHO DID NOT PRAY FOR A MIRACLE. We were no different.

As Jesse's condition continued to worsen during the spring and
summer of 2001, Tim and I earnestly prayed for divine healing, as
did thousands of others! Oh, how our hearts ached for God to act
on behalf of our son's sight and his life! We knew that He could if
He willed to. Was He listening? How could a loving God seemingly
turn a deaf ear to the cry of so many of His children? Why was He
not responding to our constant prayers with healing power? As
one might imagine, we received a myriad of answers from a variety
of sources. Some of them made us smile!

At various times some very well-meaning and often generous people declared that God would certainly heal Jesse if only we would tap into some new and amazing cure. We were offered many different so-called "miracle cures," given with great assurance that these would "heal" him, or at least purge the body's toxins and build up its immune system so that it could heal itself. "God has built into the body the capacity to heal itself," we were instructed, and we do not doubt that there was a measure of truth in this. I have a list of at least ten different products which we were either given or encouraged to buy, and many of these were said to have been developed after men had received special divine insight! That part always sounded a little mercenary!

Though we did use some of the alternative medicines we were given, we just didn't have peace about riding every new wave that came along. We sensed the Lord constantly reminding us to use good judgment and to act wisely and graciously but to place all our hopes and expectations, not in doctors, treatments or cures, but in His sovereign purpose and provision. Besides, I was so exhausted with the trips back and forth to the hospital nearly every week that trying to get my very young, cancer patient to consume a liter or two of carrot juice every morning just didn't appeal to me. (Getting that much vegetable juice down Jesse's throat would have been the greatest miracle of all!) Nor was I about to force him to sleep with magnetic blindfolds over his eyes at night, as one suggested (these were supposed to pull the cancer toxins out of his body). One interesting person told us that feeding Jesse a large amount of cow colostrum each day would most certainly wipe out the cancer tumors, but short of starting my own dairy farm I didn't think this seemed feasible either!

At the end of the day we chose traditional, modern medicine and skilled, medical professionals based upon the clear, documented statistics of this disease. The fact remains that one hundred years ago, retinoblastoma was one hundred percent fatal. Today, with modern, medical treatment, ninety-six percent of children will live. This, coupled with the peace of God, gave us confidence that we were making the right choices for treatment, and we tried not to get distracted with a million and one options.

Tim and I believe in divine healing. Some of the most precious memories we share as a family are of unforgettable, powerful moments where God has poured healing virtue upon one of us in direct response to prayer. But it's one thing to believe that God can do something and another to believe that He will do it! For the first three years, even while praying for a miracle, I think we always had an underlying sense that God was unfolding His plan—that this story was so much bigger than us. But as Jesse's condition became more and more desperate and as total blindness or even loss of life became a greater and greater possibility, we lost perspective for a little while. We began to listen to our fears. We began to listen to some extreme counsel—to entertain some deceptive doctrines. We began to think so much about faith that we began to put faith in our faith rather than faith in God. We began to question our faith. Here is where we struggled—not so much with God as with us.

As we meditated on the biblical accounts of miraculous healing, we reminded ourselves that God had not changed; that He is still a God of love and power. Nothing is too difficult for Him. We read of lame men being made whole, of a mother receiving her son back from the dead, of a leprous man's skin being made as new and soft as a child's, of a woman receiving healing virtue simply by touching Jesus' garment and of blind beggars receiving their sight. From early childhood we were taught that "Jesus Christ is the same yesterday, today, and forever."

In the heavy fog of sorrow, when the purposes of God were hidden from us, we became dangerously introspective—wrestling with questions and doubts we never thought we would wrestle with. Why wouldn't He act on our behalf as He had in so many others? Hadn't Jesus said, *"Ask, and it will be given to you; seek, and you will find; knock, and it will be opened to you"* (Matt 7:7)? Was there something broken with our faith? Were we simply not desperate enough or fervent enough in our praying? Were the Lord's hands bound by elements of unbelief or sin still remaining in us? Were we just too undisciplined in our supplications to prevail for the miracle? Were we, Jesse's parents, standing in the way of healing? Those of you who have lived through crises similar to ours will understand this fog we were in.

Sometimes, well-meaning friends added to this temptation toward unhealthy introspection. One good man, who has since gone to be with the Lord, admonished us toward heroic "faith." He said that we should go back to the Philippines and leave Jesse and his sickness in God's hands; that although Jesse's life was important, it wasn't nearly as important as the souls we would win on the field and that we must always put God first, even above our families and children. If that was faith, we were pretty sure we didn't have it!

Another day I received a troubling phone call from a well-meaning lady who, not so subtly, insinuated that Tim and I might at least be partly to blame for the fact that God had not healed Jesse. She had heard, I think, that we were praying for healing, "according to the will of the Lord," and she reacted strongly against this kind of prayer. "It is never God's will for one of His children to be sick, or blind, or deaf, or afflicted with any other disease!" she adamantly insisted. She believed that as children of God we had the right to declare and demand physical healing. She insisted that our praying "according to God's will" was symptomatic of wavering faith, faith which should never expect to receive what it asks for. In our darkness we worried that she was right, and we trembled at the thought!

Tim and I could not bear the thought that our lack of definiteness was causing God to refuse our request and the request of thousands of our friends and family members. We could not live with ourselves if our unbelief resulted in a lifetime of blindness for this little boy that we both loved so much? In this blinding mist of sorrow we worried that she was right. We knew that wavering faith is often, though not always, the cause of unanswered prayer, but we weren't sure this was our problem. Nor were we sure that it wasn't!

After this phone call, where elements of truth were so interwoven with hurtful deceptions, I was troubled. Although something in my spirit didn't agree with her spirit on this matter, I was very tempted to feel that perhaps I was going to be the cause of Jesse's demise. I was troubled for the rest of the day, going about my normal duties with the mocking voice of guilt whispering accusingly in my mind. As I cleared the supper dishes, Tim came from his office and leaned against the counter. "Hey, Becky," he began, "listen to what I have just read in the Scriptures."

Tim began reading from Mark chapter one about the leper who came to Jesus seeking healing. He emphasized these words of the leper and Jesus: *"Lord, If you are willing, you can make me clean."* *"I am willing; be cleansed," Jesus had replied (Mark 1:40, 41).* "You see, Honey," Tim said, 'If you are willing' faith, seems to be good enough faith for Jesus to heal a man! The leper wasn't rebuked for his lack of definiteness or his unbelief when he asked Jesus to heal him 'if' He was 'willing.' In fact, Jesus seems to acknowledge that the leper's theology was right by saying, 'I am willing.' In other words, 'Mr. Leper you're quite right, I do heal according to My will, and right now I will to heal you!' So, even if we're not sure of God's will, Becky, and even if we lack the definiteness we wish we had, God can still heal our son if He chooses to."

It was a moment of insight for me. Clearly this sick man had prayed for the will of God to be done in his life and left the rest up to Jesus. He turned the spotlight off of himself and shone it in on the Lord! We came to understand that we had to do this too. "For every look at self, take ten looks at Christ," said Robert Murray McCheyne. This is the only path to peace. God is pleased with our prayers of deep, inner conviction when He gives us the grace to do so, but also of relinquishment to His will—to His glory. Both conviction and relinquishment are consistent with faith. I rested for some time in this truth.

Not long after this, however, waves of self-doubt began to roll over us again. We knew we couldn't go on like this! We just had to settle this matter of healing in our hearts for good, so we decided to diligently and specifically seek the Lord together. Tim decided that he would fast a certain number of days, humbling himself before the Lord. Though I had to be a mommy to our children I agreed to join him in seeking God's will. We asked God during that week to show us our own hearts and to reveal any secret sins or hindrances to our faith. This focused time with the Lord became a very profitable time for us spiritually—especially for Tim.

Tim remembers his specific prayer to the Lord during this time. "Father," he prayed, "I don't know how to pray. I don't know what to say. Do You want to heal? Is it wrong not to know the answer to this question? And, Father," he pled, "how can we work up enough confidence to ask You for a miracle? Where do we get more faith? Is there some spiritual valve that we can turn to release the flow of Your healing power? Please, Father, give us an answer that we can rest in Your will."

One memorable day as he was communing with the Lord while walking through a lovely little pine forest near our home, God answered his questioning heart. Tim had been meditating on the crisis of Jesus' beloved friends in John chapter eleven. He found himself trying to reconcile Jesus' delay—His lack of responsiveness to the prayers of Mary and Martha for their dying brother—with His love. He wondered, "If He loved them, why did He delay 'two more days in the place where He was'? Why is He seemingly ignoring their request?" Tim found it rather easy to identify with their sorrow and confusion of heart. *"Lord, if You had been here, my brother would not have died"* (v. 21), both sisters had lamented through their tears. (Grief often yields more questions than answers).

As Tim continued to meditate upon this text, the answer suddenly became clear in the very words of Jesus. *"This sickness is not unto death, but for the glory of God, that the Son of God may be glorified through it"* (v. 4). And toward the end of this story, just before He called Lazarus out of the tomb, Jesus repeated this theme to Martha with a question, *"Did I not say to you that if you would believe you would see the glory of God?"* (v. 40).

As Tim walked under the beautiful canopy of trees the voice of the Lord began to penetrate the hardness of his heart. "My son," He spoke tenderly, "I don't want you to worry about My intentions toward Jesse or My will for your family. Nor do I want you to keep measuring your faith. What I want you to pray for right now, and the only thing I want you to pray for, is for My glory. I want you to believe that whatever I choose to do in Jesse's life and in your family, I'll be glorified through it. I want you to pray that through this difficult trial, men and women will see the embodiment of My love, My peace, My joy and My enabling grace and that by seeing Me they will be emboldened to love and trust Me more. You don't need heroic faith, son! You just need to yield everything to Me and let Me be God. This is enough for Me, son. This is all I ask from you."

Someone has said that in order to clean up a dark room one must throw open the windows and let the light in. This is what the Lord graciously did for Tim. And as the Lord spoke so clearly to his heart that day, a dam of pent up fear, emotion and doubt broke

71

loose in his mind and heart and the pure Word of God brought cleansing and absolute freedom! That day we learned the important lesson that sometimes faith is action and sometimes faith is inaction (waiting on the Lord), but always faith is surrender to God's glory. Faith does not demand of God something we want but simply trusts Him to do what He wants to do in and through us. And His grace is able to make His wants our wants.

Although we weren't granted a last-minute, miraculous healing for our Jesse, we were given something greater. We were granted the peace to accept the path that was chosen for him and for us with the unwavering assurance that God's glory would be revealed, even in what seemed unthinkable. Therein lies the miracle.

Through the most excruciating weeks and months of uncertainty, the Lord helped Tim and me to see this present world, with its mix of joy and pain, through two lenses. Through the first lens we saw the world as it ought to be and someday will be; the world of eternity where all is made new; the world where all the tearful effects of sin are wiped away; a world where pain has finally given way to perfect life. Through the second lens we learned to see, and accept, the world as it is now—a world still groaning; a world eagerly anticipating final redemption; a world where the spiritual redemption of our souls may be complete but where the redemption of our physical bodies has to wait. As the apostle Paul put it, *"We also who have the first-fruits of the Spirit, even we ourselves groan within ourselves, eagerly waiting for the adoption, the redemption of our body"* (Romans 8:23).

We've come to believe that those who look only through the first lens, but refuse to take an honest look at the second, will form a distorted image of the world and create expectations for health, wealth and prosperity never intended by the gospel. We do not now see all things as they ought to be outwardly, but by God's grace we will.

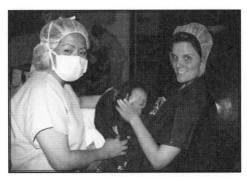

Jesse, 30 minutes old
at St. Lukes Hospital, Manila, Philippines
with Dr. Olympia and Mommy

Jesse (15 mo. old) and Daddy
getting ready for the OR
December 1998

Jesse (15 mo. old) after EUA
(exam under anesthesia)
Timothy and Valerie
were along for the ride
December 1998

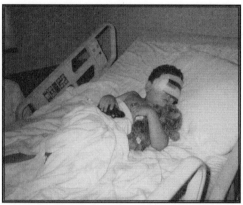

Enduring four days of blindness
after a radioactive plaque
had been sewn inside his eye

The morning of
Jesse's final surgery
September 10, 2001

Jesse in the hospital
after losing his second eye
September 2001

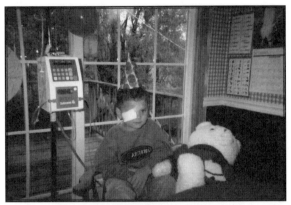

Jesse's 4th Birthday Party
September 2001

Jesse trying his new cane
December 2001

Typing his ABC's on his
new Perkins Brailler

Enjoying his new Jeep

Jesse gets to hold a baby alligator

Tim and Jesse building a sand castle
at the South China Sea

Jesse with little sisters,
Carolyn and Samantha, in the Philippines

Jesse with his beloved Ate Mye

Jesse riding his new tri-bike with friends.
Yes, he's the driver!

A Fun Day visiting 100 islands in the Philippines
with Tim Jr. and friend, Stephen

Jesse and his siblings on the beach
in Puerto Galero, Mindoro Philippines

Jesse with Samantha, at their joint graduations,
His 8th grade, her kindergarten

Jesse water skiing

The Keep Family

Jesse

CHAPTER SIX

―――◄❧►―――

The Bedrock of Truth

*"And you shall know the truth,
and the truth shall make you free."*
John 8:32

TIM AND I WERE BOTH RAISED IN DEVOUT CHRISTIAN HOMES. From our earliest memories we were taught to believe that the Scriptures are God-breathed; that they are infallible and reliable, and we were continually admonished to read them, memorize them and obey them. But the destructive winds and waves of crises beating upon our little household presented us with an opportunity to experience their stabilizing power like nothing else could have.

As we journeyed with Jesse through the years of treatment we began to seek counsel and strength from the Word of God as we never had. Could it be counted on to sustain us in the situation that we were now in? Is it really true that *"all things work together for good to those who love God, to those who are the called according to His purpose"* (Romans 8:28)? Is it true that, *"even in darkness, light dawns for the upright"* (Psalm 112:4 NIV)?

EYES TO SEE

It was as if our family stood at the edge of a vast, deep canyon peering down into a net designed by God to catch us when we fell. We had stood there our whole lives, declaring our confidence in the integrity of that net, but we had never fallen … that far! Experience had not forged our beliefs into convictions. But this was to change. Suddenly, and without warning, we were pushed off that edge and into the dark, mysterious unknown. Would the Word of God prove strong to save us now? Would it hold us? Were the Scriptures able to preserve our joy in God, our love, our family and our eternal hope? We discovered that it was during the fearful free fall—that out-of-our-control place between the edge and the net—that Satan often mocked us and tried to destroy our faith! And we found that the free fall was not fun. At times we seemed to be flailing in fear and, yes, even unbelief. But I'm so thankful that no natural emotion or attack of the enemy could compromise the truth or strength of that net! We found that God is absolutely and unchangeably a God of truth.

We continued constant and varied treatments in an attempt to permanently destroy the tumors affecting Jesse's right eye. Just when we thought he was "cancer free for good" we'd be hit with the devastating news that another tumor had cropped up. It was in July of 2001 that Dr. Roarty looked at us with both honesty and compassion in his eyes and delivered this not-so-subtle message, "You both need to keep in mind that life is more important than sight."

I recoiled inwardly at these words! We knew intellectually what he was gently trying to prepare us for, but our hearts were slow to accept it. How could it have come to this? We had prayed and even fasted for Jesse's sight to be spared, and thousands had prayed with us. Blindness just didn't make sense. The prospect of our son being blind was mind numbing, and yet we began to try to prepare ourselves for what lay ahead.

THE BEDROCK OF TRUTH

It was a sweet summer filled with memories that will forever be imprinted upon my heart. We took long nature walks, turning over rocks to look at the creepy crawlies that lay underneath. The grass had never looked greener or the flowers more beautiful as I began to really see and appreciate the loveliness of the world around me. I felt an almost frantic urgency to "show" Jesse the magnificent wonders surrounding him. We took multiple trips to the zoo. It was important to me that my son know what an elephant, a giraffe and a monkey looked like. We were painfully aware of the fact that Jesse's vision was slipping away and were tormented by the knowledge that we could do nothing to stop it from happening.

Driving home after one particularly long day in Detroit, and yet another discouraging report, Tim pulled off the Brighten exit on I-96. He took Jesse into a Meijer store and walked straight to the toy section. I stood back and watched as my husband bought a two-hundred and fifty dollar, battery-operated jeep. He was a man on a mission! The knowledge that Jesse would never drive a car had compelled a quite un-impulsive man to do a very impulsive thing. He wanted his son to have the experience of driving.

It was a happy evening at our house, and both our boys, Tim Jr. and Jesse, danced around the kitchen, their eyes brimming with excitement as they watched Daddy assemble the jeep. The following day, we sat outside and drank in the sight of the boys zooming around our yard in that ridiculously over-priced, impulsively acquired contraption. But I'll forever cherish the memory of their happy faces—Timothy's toothless grin and Jesse's curly head thrown back as he let out a delightful belly laugh that was loud and distinctly his.

In early June our friends, George and Linda Kelly, loaned us their cabin which was situated right on the shores of Lake Superior. We spent a week strolling along the beach, collecting beautiful rocks and comparing our footprints in the sand. Tim and I took early morning walks along the lake. In that tranquil place, surrounded by the breathtaking beauty of the lakeshore, I would talk to God and Him to me. I felt His presence, and my hopeless worries were washed away like the sand as I communed with Him. My perspective was adjusted, and hope rose in my heart with the morning sun.

Truly, it was an idyllic week; the children played the days away building castles and burying each other in the sugar sand. They flirted with the frigid water along the edge of Lake Superior, daring one another to stick their feet in. We roasted marshmallows over a bonfire and allowed the kids to stay up long past their bedtime to watch the eleven o'clock sunsets.

During one late evening walk on the beach, Jesse exclaimed, "Mommy, look, it's doing it again." I looked up and watched as the deep orange of the sun melted into the horizon, casting a brilliant canopy of color over the lake and the northern sky. It took my breath away, and then came the crushing knowledge that he was very possibly watching one of the last sunsets that he would ever see. Jesse was oblivious to my morose thoughts and a moment later was running as fast as he could along the beach singing at the top of his lungs, "This is a goooood day!"

In August of 2001, just a few weeks after our time at the lake, Jesse had his first experience with total blindness. In a very last ditch effort to annihilate the tumors in his remaining eye, Dr. Roarty went in and sewed a radioactive plaque onto the tumor. Jesse's eye had to be covered for four days with a lead lined patch. He was devastated! He laid there desperately trying to be brave, his lip quivering, clutching a new matchbox car in one hand and a pack of gum in the other. He was silent except to say, "Mommy, its dark." Valerie and Tim Jr. made cassette tapes of themselves, telling stories and being silly. We would play these for Jesse to pass the time. Tim and I reassured him constantly that this would only be for four days; that in four days, they would remove the patch and then he would be able to see again. This gave both him and us a measure of comfort, but we agonized as we watched him—our three year old—have to deal with this terrifying trauma.

We had to make valiant attempts to keep our happy faces on for Jesse's benefit, but inside we were dying! I wrote the following in my journal on the second day of this treatment:

> *"I have been crying out to God tonight. I just cannot reconcile this with 'Good'! How can this be good? My faith feels unbelievably weak! I feel terrified!"*

Jesse, with his tough resilience, and the amazing grace of God, did recover and actually became his playful self again, even while he was still patched. We were exuberant and so thankful for this miracle. I will never forget that day when they removed the patch, and his swollen, irradiated eye opened just enough for him to be able to see. He jumped off the bed throwing his arms around my neck and exclaimed, "I can see Mommy! I can see you!" It was an unforgettable moment of joy, and we prayed and hoped that this treatment would destroy this cancer for good.

Our joy was heightened when one week later Dr. Roarty told us that this treatment appeared to be working. By now, however, I was living day to day with fear perched on my shoulder, whispering in my ear at every opportune moment and constantly threatening to destroy my peace. I vacillated between a fervent trust in who I knew God to be, based upon His Word, and the uncertainty of Jesse's future. On my best days, I was ready to face anything, confident in the fact that God's grace would carry us through. I would write in my journal, *"I'm desperately clinging to my faith in our all wise God. Surely He hasn't left us."* And on my worst, I would write things such as the following, written in a letter to my friend and mentor, Cathy Parker, in August of 2001: *"I feel like we're taking a huge test, one that has lasted for almost four years, and that I'm about to flunk!"* I praise God that His truth and goodness aren't based upon our emotions.

On a Thursday afternoon, September 6, 2001, Dr. Roarty walked through the door of the family waiting room, and from the grim look on his face I knew that we were in for some bad news. We sat in silent dread as he crouched down, and sitting on his heels in front of us began, "Things aren't good. The tumor which has caused Jesse so many problems lately is growing and pressing on his optic nerve, and this eye needs to come out now!" Dr. Roarty had become more than just a doctor to Tim and me. He was a trusted friend. As he spoke, he was professional, but we knew that this was a painful blow to him as well, and in ten years of treating this disease, he had only had one other patient with retinoblastoma to lose both eyes. We asked him if we could have the weekend to prepare ourselves (as if we could), and he consented.

We left the hospital that day in silent resignation. The return trip was a quiet one, for we didn't want to talk in front of Jesse just yet. As we neared our home, he unbuckled his seat belt and leaned forward. "You know what I feel like doing?" he said, "I feel like painting a picture!" We had been home only a few minutes when he reminded me, "Mommy, I want to paint."

I walked into the kitchen, rummaged around in a drawer, finally finding some finger-paint and a piece of blank paper for a canvas. I put an apron on Jesse and left him at the table happily painting away. I forgot about him until he called me back to the kitchen to see his artistic masterpiece. As I peered over his shoulder to see what my budding Michelangelo had created, he looked up at me with that expectant look that every parent understands; the one that expects you to recognize just what they've painted! I racked my brain and tried to imagine something—anything—in the dark, smeared blob of colors. But try as I might, I simply could not.

He gave up on me and with an exasperated tone said, "Mommy, it's a rainbow … a messy rainbow!" I couldn't see the rainbow, but because he was the artist he had no trouble seeing it. I placed the childish work of art on top of the refrigerator to dry, and there it remained, forgotten and untouched, for several weeks.

During that difficult weekend, Tim and I wrestled with how to talk with Jesse (and his siblings as well) about what was going to happen on Monday. We knew we wanted this conversation. Some may say that this was foolish, but we felt that it was only fair to prepare our son as best we could. I wondered aloud to Tim, "How do you tell an almost four-year-old, little boy that he is going to be blind." He had no answer for me, of course. There was no "right" answer. It felt so surreal … so heavy … so wrong.

Jesse was smart. Weeks earlier, after having obviously overheard one of our "parent only" conversations, he had exhibited some of his "childish understanding" of the way things might turn out for him. While swinging happily at the park with his then ten-year-old sister, Valerie, he had suddenly piped up with, "Sissy, some kids are blind." "That's right Jesse," she had replied. He continued, "I might be blind too, but for now … I want to see for the whole week!" We found some sad humor in this but knew very well that "the whole week" to a three year old simply meant a very, very long time.

Tim and I sat him down on Saturday afternoon, and using his previous experience of blindness as a reference point, we told him that his eye was really sick. We explained to him that Dr. Roarty needed to take this eye out so that the rest of his body would not become sick. After our weak and very inadequate "talk," He simply looked at us and said, quite matter-of-factly, "I don't want to do that." With that, he jumped off the couch and ran outside. We didn't even try to follow it up with further discussion. It was so overwhelming. We had never read a book on parenting which could have prepared us for these challenges. We were sailing in rough, uncharted waters so we simply prayed and did the best we could.

On Monday morning, September 10, 2001, Jesse awoke to his last day of sight in this world. We were blessed to be surrounded by friends and family as we took him to Children's Hospital in Detroit, Michigan. Pastor Jones and his wife Saundy were there too. At the close of the day Blake would offer the following reflection in a letter written to our church family and mission supporters:

> Dear friends,
>
> It is late in the evening but I thought you might be interested in how Jesse Keep's day has progressed.
>
> First, his surgery was postponed until about three forty-five p.m., and so the family was able to hold him and talk with his rather subdued, little self for most of the afternoon. There were about twenty-one of us there all together ... Periodically, someone of the staff would stop by to share their love with the Keeps.
>
> Finally Jesse was carried into pre-op, and of course, the whole ordeal was laden with such finality ... the family stood in the hall in a huddle and wept together.

THE BEDROCK OF TRUTH

We looked on in broken helplessness ...

Likely, Jesse will be sent home tomorrow with a big patch on his eyes. His daddy bought him a puppy last weekend, so Jesse will be able to hold "Buddy." I reckon he will need his little furry friend. Some friends from Vandercook Bible Methodist Church sent cowboy boots for Jesse, so they will stop by our home to pick them up tomorrow.

Timothy and Valerie have shared the grief in this grueling day. May the loving Heavenly Father hold them in His arms tonight as well as little Jesse.

No doubt, as I write this, Becky is holding Jesse close to herself in his hospital bed. He will have morphine for the intense pain tonight. Becky had trouble sleeping last night, and tomorrow may be long, long! Please pray for her. The uncertainty of the future and the question of new cancer development leaves her pretty disturbed, naturally.

God's grace is working in [Tim and Becky's] lives, but the enemy will use these days to flog them with questions and taunts. Please, please hold them close to the throne of grace in your prayers. God will bring them through. And no doubt, the Eternal One sees the bigger picture and rich and eternal value in what He has allowed to happen today. We trust Him for He makes no mistakes ....

Thanks for your prayers today,
Blake Jones

EYES TO SEE

As we pulled into Detroit Children's Hospital parking garage for the seventieth time (at least), I realized that we were traversing the last and most difficult hill of this four-year roller coaster ride of cancer. Tim and I had signed consent papers many times before, but I remember standing with pen in hand and reading the form much more slowly now before signing my name to the document that would allow the "enucleation" of our little boy's right eye. That word looked harsh and ugly on the page.

My heart ached as I watched Jesse and his best buddy, Cousin David, take turns looking through a viewfinder in the surgery waiting area. This was something that I had taken for granted so many times before, but today it filled me with profound sadness.

The nurses who had taken care of Jesse so many times informed Tim and me that they had "fixed" the one-parent-only rule and that we would both be allowed to go back to the OR with Jesse until he was sedated. We had taken turns doing this more than seventy times before, but today was different. We knew that when he closed his eyes on this day, his world would remain forever dark. We wanted our faces to be the last that he would see. It was very emotional for both of us. I looked up and watched as the anesthesiologist placed a small mask over Jesse's nose and mouth through which flowed the bubble-gum scented gas that quickly closed his eyes. As she did so, I saw tears running down her face and into her surgical mask. I knew that she was empathizing with our hearts in that moment. This was not just another "case" for these wonderful doctors and nurses. This was a little boy on whom they had all exercised their highest expertise in order to cure, and they had become like family to our family. They had fought tirelessly for years to save his life and his sight. We were, and are, so grateful for each of them and thankful that our son's life was spared.

THE BEDROCK OF TRUTH

A few hours later, Tim and I found ourselves standing next to the bedside of our still anesthetized little boy. The upper part of his head was swathed in bandages, but I could still see the thick shock of curly hair poking out from underneath. The nurses had carefully tucked his favorite blanket around him, and his Sesame Street friend "Ernie" was lying faithfully by his side.

Tim and I were glad that he was sleeping and couldn't see us as we stood there crying. Honestly, I wasn't thinking about God's goodness, or His truthfulness, or sovereignty in that moment. I was overcome with the finality of what had taken place. How in the world were we going to raise a blind child? We knew nothing about blindness. What would his life be like now? Would he be the same happy, fun-loving child that we knew? What would he be when he grew up? How would he make it in the world with this disability thrust upon him? It was then that I felt an arm around my shoulder and heard my dad's familiar voice. He drew Tim and me close to him and whispered through his own tears, "Tim … Becky, there is something that you need to remember right now … something you must never forget." He continued, "God is still good!" I heard the catch in his voice as he repeated it over and over, "God is still good … God is still good."

In that moment, in spite of our torn and bleeding hearts, we made a deliberate choice to submit our minds to the truth of that statement! God's Word is true, and He is the "Good Shepherd." His goodness had led us safely to this place with our faith and family intact. His goodness would no doubt lead us through the difficult and uncertain days ahead. Because He is good, He has promised us in His Word that He will one day wipe away every tear from our eyes and that there will be no more sorrow, crying, cancer, divorce, death, blindness, or any other trouble which is so much a part of our human story. Because God's Word is true, we can rejoice when we read verses like, *"In this world, you will have trouble. But take heart! I have overcome the world"* (John 16:33).

My husband and I were blessed to be surrounded by people, such as my father, who understood our grief and yet gently redirected our gaze from momentary affliction to timeless truth. We were reminded in that moment that focusing on the truth about God would empower us to face the uncertain future, not without anxiety, but with certain hope.

I rediscovered Jesse's "rainbow" art again on one of the most difficult days following his surgery. The tears flowed as I remembered the day that Jesse had painted it—this very last work of art as a sighted, little boy. I also recalled vividly our conversation that day, and it struck me powerfully that my life in that moment seemed just like this picture—an unsightly mixture of colors and dark blotches on a canvas. I could see the "messy" all right, but I couldn't see a rainbow; I couldn't imagine anything beautiful. Our son was blind, and he would never see again. How could this ever be a thing of beauty? What was God thinking when He brushed this pain onto the canvas of our lives … on Jesse's life? The details were all mixed up, and I could see nothing lovely or valuable in God's artistry.

This painting now hangs in my kitchen so that I might never forget the timeless truth that was emblazoned on my heart through the power of the Holy Spirit as He gently said to me, "Becky, your Heavenly Father, the Creator of your life's painting, can indeed see what you cannot. He sees a rainbow you cannot see, and you need only trust His wisdom and His love." I know with certainty that the God of the Universe, the One who cannot lie, used the finger painting of a three-year-old little boy—the "messy rainbow"—to remind me of His promise that He would never leave me, and that His grace was and will always be sufficient.

CHAPTER SEVEN

---❦---

Is Jesus Crying?

"His is a loving, tender hand,
full of sympathy and compassion."
D. L. Moody

We felt constant ministrations of love from many wonderful people during Jesse's four-year battle with cancer. God's people—our friends and supporters—prayed for us and sent cards of encouragement and financial support which overwhelmed us at times. We experienced the Spirit of Christ's love and compassion as we never had before.

For instance, our children received so many gifts over the years that we had to work pretty hard as parents at not allowing them to become spoiled by all the attention. I remember Jesse's fourth birthday, which was shortly after his last surgery. He received seventy-five gifts in the mail from people all over the United States. He began to anticipate the mailman each day. It was not only fun but also eased a little of the stress during that time. We all got a good laugh one day after Jesse received (just after having his last eye removed) a cute stuffed dinosaur. The kids discovered that if they squeezed him his eyes would bulge way out of their sockets. It was kind of creepy, but we were humored at the appropriate, inappropriateness of this gift. Jesse thought it was cool. We discovered just how vital God's people are during times of suffering—just being the earthly, human hands and feet of Jesus to the hurting.

The morning after Jesse's remaining eye was removed, they discharged him, and we took him home. I was more than a little nervous about it. He was physically fine I guess—maybe I was not ready to be responsible for this newly blind child.

It was a particularly difficult morning as we prepared to leave the hospital. It was an infamous day, not only for us but for the world. It was September 11, 2001. I was lying in the bed with Jesse, trying to console him as he lamented over the fact that he could not see, when the phone rang. I answered and heard my sister Vicky's stressed and anxious voice. She told me to turn on the TV. When we did we witnessed the horrifying events of that morning. We were in the midst of our own personal tragedy but realized that another was taking place on a much larger scale, and with far greater ramifications. A new and different kind of fear sliced through me like a knife as I watched the fiery inferno of the World Trade Center and Pentagon. I finally pleaded with Tim to turn it off! I couldn't cope with Jesse and what felt like the end of the world at the same time. The hospital went into lockdown mode, and a pall settled in over the whole place, as it did over our entire country and the world that morning.

We left the hospital and went to my sister Julia's house in Concord, Michigan. She and her husband Dave had been caring for Valerie and Timothy during Jesse's hospital stay. Wanting to watch the news together, we decided to spend the night there. It was comforting to be with family on this day. Our emotions were raw, and we were exhausted.

I watched as Jesse tried his best to play with his cousins that evening; they were all so sweet, tiptoeing around him as if they feared that he would break. Pain squeezed my heart as I lay on the couch, quietly observing the children and wondering how this would affect their relationship with Jesse. My mind wandered to many previous nights like this one when Jesse and David Jr. had run through the house freely, screaming like banshees till Julia and I were sorely tempted to hog-tie and sedate both of them. Would he play with such uninhibited abandon again—would things ever be the same?

Jesse awakened at three o'clock a.m. screaming, but unable to articulate to us what the problem was. "Mommy," he finally said through his tears, "Call Dr. Roarty and tell him not to do the surgery." I sat on the stairway holding Jesse and feeling paralyzed by helplessness. Tim and I tried everything to console him. We prayed. We gave him a warm bath. We even called Dr. Roarty at 3:30 in the morning, waking him up just to hear his voice and ask for advice. Jesse finally yelled, "Just get me out of here!" Instant understanding flowed into my heart and mind—he desperately wanted out of the dark place that he was in. How we longed in that moment to rescue him from that place and grieved at our inability to do so.

Feeling that we had to do something—anything to distract Jesse— we decided to go for a drive. Tim carried him to the car and the three of us—all in our pajamas—started out. We drove for a long time but with no destination in mind. I laid in the backseat with Jesse in my arms until at last he fell into an exhausted sleep. We were bone-weary, but rather than risk waking him, Tim and I decided to spend the rest of the night in the car. I dozed fitfully on the uncomfortable seat, but Jesse's peaceful sleep was worth far more to me than a warm bed.

We did not share this story outside of our immediate family, but a few weeks later we received a letter from Tim's Aunt Molly. She wanted us to know that on the night of September 11, she had been suddenly awakened with the strong impression that we were having a very difficult night, and that she was to get out of bed and pray for us. She obeyed, and we were amazed to realize that as we were driving around aimlessly with a suffering child, God was sitting up and taking notice. And out of His heart of compassion, He used one of His children as an instrument through whom He could pour out His grace upon us.

One of the things that I dreaded the most was the conversation that I knew was coming when Jesse awakened from surgery. In the days leading up to the surgery, Tim and I prayed earnestly for wisdom to answer the difficult questions he was sure to ask. After all, parents are supposed to be there to comfort and ease the pain of their children. We are the ones who assure and reassure our kids that everything will be "okay." I wasn't even at the place where my sweet little boy being blind was "okay." How in the world was I going to truthfully help him through this? It seemed so wrong to have to offer such harsh reality to a three-year-old.

I was sleeping fitfully in a chair beside Jesse's bed when somewhere in the wee hours of the morning I heard his hoarse little voice call out to me.

"Mommy."

"Yes, Jesse," I replied, "Mommy is right here."

IS JESUS CRYING?

"Mommy," he said, "I can't see."

I climbed into the bed beside him and gathered him up in my arms. There were no appropriate words that I could think of to reply to his solemn declaration. I reminded him gently about his eye being "sick" and how Dr. Roarty had to take it out. I did not want to have this conversation! I tried to get him back to sleep, but his bright, three-year-old mind was buzzing with questions.

He went on, "But mommy, how am I going to ride my bike? How will I go up the stairs? I can't walk on the stairs if I can't see. And, Mommy, I can't swing high anymore if I can't see."

This went on for some time as his mind went into overdrive thinking of all the things that he would not be able to do without his sight. Overwhelmed with emotion and fighting back tears, I reassured him that we would figure these things out. We would figure a way for him to ride his bike, climb the stairs, and swing high on the swings.

"Mommy," Jesse said hopefully, "is this just going to be for four days?"

I knew that he was remembering his four-day stint with blindness the month before, and I cringed as I recalled how Tim and I had promised him repeatedly, "Jesse, after four days you will be able to see." This was a sad memory to me, for now, I had no such good news to tell him. I also remembered my conversation with him on that night ... his first true night of blindness—the previous month when he had been patched for four days. He had been upset; he was asking me why he couldn't see. He was telling me all the things that he would no longer be able to do without his sight on that night as well. I was crying quietly and trying to hide it from him, but suddenly he asked, "Mommy, are you sad?"

"Yes, Jesse, Mommy is sad," I replied.

He was quiet for a moment, and then His next question nearly stopped my heart,

"Mommy."

"Yes, Jesse."

"Is Jesus Crying?"

I paused, letting this question sink into my brain. A torrent of certainty washed over me a moment later, and I answered him quietly, but confidently, "Yes, Jesse, I believe that He is crying with us tonight." For you see, I had read the story, many times in my life, of a Jesus who wept with Mary and Martha at the death of their brother. I had memorized as a child those words in Hebrews 4:15 which say, *"For we do not have a high priest who is unable to sympathize with our weakness but we have one who was tempted in every way such as we and yet without sin."* I have since learned that this means that He, the God of the universe, counts our miseries as His own.

As I held my young son in my arms on this most difficult night, and as we grieved together over his loss, I was acutely aware of a God in heaven who was very connected and was somehow even participating in our sorrow. I felt the compassion of my heavenly Father and with it, His comfort and peace.

CHAPTER EIGHT

---❧---

The Best Healing of All

*We are not necessarily doubting that God will do what's best for us;
we are only wondering how painful the best will turn out to be.*
C. S. Lewis

VERY OFTEN THE GREATEST HEALING IS NOT A MIRACULOUS
DELIVERANCE FROM DISEASE, but rather the healing of one's heart.

We had just come through four harrowing years of fighting for
Jesse's sight and his life. Now we had lost the battle for his eyesight.
Tim and I were exhausted and felt that surely we had been pressed to
the very limit of our human endurance. We were ready for a heavenly relief team to pour out the warm oil of healing over our hearts and
restore our lives to some semblance of order. This was not to be the
case for a time as God had yet another dimension of His greatness to
demonstrate to us, and this would only be realized through the most
painful days that were still ahead for Jesse and for us.

After Jesse's final surgery, we took him home and sought to live life as normally as possible. I soon realized how many things would be different. Some things were minimal and even a little humorous. I realized just how inconvenient it was for Jesse when someone forgot to put their shoes away. He was always tripping and falling over things left carelessly around. In exasperation one day, I told the kids that the next person to leave their shoes in the middle of the floor would be blindfolded for an hour. This worked great until Jesse tripped over his own shoes. He took my scolding in stride and quipped, "Well, Mommy, you can't blindfold me; I'm already blindfolded!" He had a point!

I won't forget walking past Jesse's bedroom door one Sunday afternoon and seeing him lying on his stomach with his favorite books in front of him. He slowly turned the pages lingering over each one as if he were reading every word. I asked him what he was doing, and he replied solemnly, "I'm reading my books." I wondered what he was thinking about but didn't ask. It broke my heart. Then there was the night when he insisted that we leave his light on. I tried to reason with him, reminding him that "We always turn the light off when we sleep." He became very agitated and insistent that the light be left on. Tim and I decided to acquiesce to his desire. He immediately calmed down and went to sleep. Though he couldn't see the light, the mere knowledge that it was on was comforting to him.

Only a few days after coming home from the hospital, we noticed that Jesse began to withdraw. He lost interest in play and wanted to sit for hours on the couch each day listening to stories on tape. I remember one story in particular that he wanted to play over and over again. It was a tragic story about a young boy who had been hit by a train. I'm sure that it had a character building purpose in it somewhere, but Jesse was fixated on it. We were concerned and finally just put it away.

Jesse moved from sadness to anger. The tears came and the incessant questions began! "Mommy, am I going to be able to see on my birthday?" "Am I going to be able to see at Christmas?" "Can Timothy see?" "That's not fair," he would wail. "How come Timothy can see but I can't see?" And then the tantrums would start. He would dissolve into tears and screaming while Tim and I stood miserably by, feeling helpless. There was not a shred of human consolation that we could offer. He didn't want to hear about all the things that we would teach him to do; He didn't want more toys or anything that we could give him materially. He wanted to see! He could think of nothing else.

One afternoon, I found Jesse curled up under our sofa table. He was miserable and complained of a severe headache. I immediately phoned the doctor who instructed me to remove Jesse's bandage while he stayed on the line. I was horrified at what lay underneath. We rushed him back to Children's hospital where they discovered that He had a serious post-surgical infection in the eye socket. He was admitted back into the hospital for what would be weeks of very strong antibiotics. He was a very ill little boy physically and also emotionally. Feeling totally overwhelmed one night after yet another angry outburst, I foolishly told Tim that I felt that we had made a serious mistake in allowing the eye to be removed. "We should have let this cancer take his life," I said. In that moment I felt that what he was experiencing now was worse than death. It seemed that the pain of watching him suffer was more than either of us could bear.

Tim and I took turns staying in the room with him while the other would spend the night next door at the Ronald McDonald House. One late evening I left Tim with Jesse and went to our room in an effort to get some much needed rest. Sleep was elusive, however, and I lay for what seemed like hours watching the red numbers turn, ever so slowly, on the digital clock next to me. "Would this night never end?"

Finally, weary of tossing, I turned on the TV in hopes of finding something—anything—to divert my tormented thoughts. It was depressing. It seemed that most channels were fixated on terror, war, and replaying the awful images of September 11 over and over. As I watched, my heart raced with anxiety. I pondered all that was happening. Not only was our son suffering, but our country was in turmoil. We were all living every day in fear of more attacks, and talk of war was everywhere. It was all so overwhelming! Where was God in all of this? And Jesse? He was not taking this blindness sitting down. Was this going to destroy him? I recalled the words that I had recently read in *"A Path through Suffering,"* written by Elisabeth Elliot. She had quoted the famous missionary Amy Carmichael who had said that "in acceptance lieth peace." I had tried to accept this and felt that in some measure I had. I realized, however, that I was not the one who had been plunged into darkness and that I could not accept this for Jesse. How I wanted God to grant him this acceptance and peace.

I walked the halls of the Ronald McDonald House at three a.m., my heart doing flip flops in my chest as I cried out to God. Finally, the weariness in every limb of my body compelled me back to my room; I climbed into bed and reached for my Bible. I was drawn to the Psalms where I read, *"Be still and know that I am God"* (Psalm 46:10). As I meditated on those words, there came a gentle and yet powerful understanding that although I didn't know how in the world we could make it through another day, God was still God and He was in control. In those moments of quiet reflection, my anxiety ebbed away—peace came, and I slept.

Jesse continued his stay in the hospital receiving four powerful infusions of IV antibiotics daily in an effort to destroy the infection in his body. He turned four while there, and the nurses brought him a birthday cake.

One evening, feeling claustrophobic in the small room, we decided to hook his IV up to a little red wagon and go for a stroll down the hall. At first, Jesse seemed to be having a good time and enjoying the outing. A few minutes into his wagon ride, however, he began asking the infamous questions. "Mommy, am I going to be able to see on my birthday?" When we answered him truthfully, he pressed on, "What about at Christmas, will I be able to see then?" And on and on it went until our barely four-year-old son was a pitiful, sobbing, bundle of anger, wailing over and over, "I want to see! I want to see!"

Tim and I had tried to be strong, we had tried to placate him and say all the right things about God and heaven and Jesus, but we stood on this evening with nothing left to say. Each futile question asked by Jesse only intensified the brutal truth that we had given and depleted our emotional energy. Our hearts were shredded to bits. We were at the end of our human abilities to handle this for even one more moment! We stopped the little red wagon right there in the hallway, and fighting back tears, we began to pray. Tim gently placed his hands on Jesse's head while I cried out to the Lord. "Father," I began, "we accept your will and our son's blindness, but Father we don't accept this! We are asking You, in Jesus' name, to please heal Jesse's heart." It was very simple but the most heartfelt and honest prayer that we had ever prayed. It was a prayer of desperate faith for desperate days. Lettie Cowman said that "the only alternative to desperate faith is despair." We were nearing the point of despair, but Praise God for desperate faith.

The very next day, I decided to take Jesse to the hospital playroom. Tim took the opportunity to grab a quick lunch at the cafeteria. Jesse was busy at the Lego table and seemed to be having a good time. There was a cute little African American boy playing with him. He looked long and hard at Jesse's face covered in bandages, and then looking at me, he asked, "Can he see?" I cringed, thinking, "Not again, let's not bring this up right now." Before I could come up with an appropriate reply however, Jesse piped up. "Nope, I'm not ever going to see again, but when I get to heaven, I'm gonna see." I was too stunned to speak so kept silent. Jesse then turned his head toward me and said, "Mommy, it's okay if I can't see." I sat speechless as he continued playing happily. When his daddy walked into the room ten minutes later Jesse immediately said, "Daddy, its okay if I can't see."

It was as if the Lord Jesus Himself had entered that playroom and sat down at a Lego table beside a little boy with a sorely wounded heart. I can see Him with His arm draped about Jesse's shoulder as He miraculously, and in a moment of time, granted the sweet release from anger and filled Jesse's heart with acceptance and peace. And, from that moment until today, He has never wasted one more moment of sorrow on his blindness. Our all-compassionate God thoroughly and completely healed his heart, and in that instance turned the setback of blindness into a set up for the rest of his life.

We were overwhelmed on that afternoon, and I still am today. As I write these words eleven years later, I rejoice to know, with certainty, that God is a God of healing power. This power is especially seen in those situations when things aren't "fixed" but rather when we are fixed—when our focus is changed from anger or even sad resignation, to true acceptance, joy and anticipation for the future, a future which includes the very thing that we once viewed as incompatible with happiness. The Word of God is true when it says, *"And God is faithful; He will not let you be tempted beyond what you can bear. But when you are tempted, he will also provide a way out so that you can endure it"* (I Corinthians 1:13 NIV). That "way out" for us this time was the grace that freed our young son from anger and opened the door to acceptance and joy.

CHAPTER NINE

---◀❧▶---

God Gets the Glory

*And His disciples asked Him, saying,
"Rabbi, who sinned, this man or his parents,
that he was born blind?"*

*Jesus answered, "Neither this man nor his parents sinned,
but that the works of God should be revealed in him."*
John 9:2-3

ON SEPTEMBER 6, 2001, four days before Jesse entered the world of blindness, Tim wrote the following letter to some of our friends and supporters.

> Dear Brothers and Sisters,
>
> I hardly know what to write but I know that you will understand. It looks as though the four-year battle for Jesse's sight is winding down. Today we received the disappointing news that a tumor has been discovered on his optic nerve and there may not be anything else that can be done except removal of the eye.

Because of this new growth, the situation has become quite serious and apart from Divine intervention Jesse will be scheduled for an enucleation (removal of the eye) as early as Monday, September tenth.

This is obviously a very difficult thing for all of our family, both immediate and extended, and as you receive this news I'm sure that you who have carried this burden with us will also feel some of the pain in your own heart. But please allow me this opportunity to remind us all that "The Battle belongs to the Lord."

The Lord Jesus Christ has given us His witness that if we will believe "We will see the Glory of God."

Love,
Tim

These words did not come easily for Tim, and only two days later, after doing all that he could for his family, he felt that he had to get alone with the Lord. He desperately felt the need to wait before Him; to fortify his faith for the difficult journey ahead. He closed himself into our bedroom and began talking to God.

"Lord," He began, "I'm a daddy. How can I bear to carry this son whom I love so much into the operating room knowing that in this life he will not see our faces again and never enjoy another sunset or look at the stars in wonder? Father, I must hear from You! Don't hide yourself now! Please give me something from Your Word upon which we can stand in the days to come."

As Tim waited on the Lord that afternoon, God took him deep into the pages of the Old Testament and to the dramatic story of Abraham's obedient offering of Isaac upon an altar. He traveled step by step with weary Abraham as he journeyed with resignation toward the place of sacrifice God had chosen. He hiked with him and Isaac up the mountain, helped them build the altar, helped Abraham lift the knife, and marveled at such faith and surrender.

As Tim pondered this story the Lord made these words live in his heart:

> *"By Myself I have sworn, says the LORD, because you have done this thing, and have not withheld your son, your only son—blessing I will bless you, and multiplying I will multiply your descendants as the stars of the heaven and as the sand which is on the seashore; and your descendants shall possess the gate of their enemies" (Genesis 22: 16, 17).*

The Lord seemed to whisper to my husband's heart, "Son, whatever My children offer up to Me in faith I will turn into blessing and even a means of redemptive hope for others. What I'm asking you and Becky to do is to trust Me with what you can't presently see and to lay your much loved son on My altar. If you will, I'll promise you blessing in the days to come."

As God became Yahweh Yireh (The Lord our Provider) to Abraham and his descendants through obedience, so He became Yahweh Yireh to us through obedience!

As I told you in the previous chapter, Jesse was readmitted to the hospital about two weeks after his blindness due to a serious post-surgical infection in the socket of the eye that had been removed.

It was a most difficult time. Thankfully, we had family who came and stayed with our two older children as this was a situation that required Tim and I to both be with Jesse. He was in pain, very ill and just miserable with it all.

One afternoon we were surprised when two of the nurses from same day surgery came up to see us. They had taken care of Jesse numerous times over the previous four years. They came bearing gifts—gifts for Jesse, gifts for me, and a beautiful card signed by the OR nurses. There was money that they had collected with the instructions, "Tim, you are to take your wife out to dinner." We were so overwhelmed and touched by their thoughtfulness.

As these nurses sat talking with us, one of the girls began to cry. She said, "God sent you to us." Tim and I sat silently not knowing what to say. She continued, "Every morning that you walked into same day surgery, you brought Jesus into that place!" Honestly, we were humbled and maybe even a little puzzled by these words. My recollection of those days didn't include feeling especially spiritual or that either of us was manifesting the Glory of God in those moments. I had a very clear memory, however, of two very tired, sleep-deprived, and coffee overloaded parents. I remembered them wearily carrying a small grumpy and very hungry little boy into a place where he would be poked, prodded, and would have to "do the mask" (his description of the application of anesthesia). I had a very clear recollection of feeling overwhelmed and anxious, not knowing what the day would bring. I recalled that Tim and I would often pray beforehand, asking God and each other for forgiveness for our impatience and irritability with one another. Could Christ be seen and God glorified in the middle of even this? My idea of God receiving glory had been more along the lines of a last minute miraculous healing of Jesse—one that was undeniably divine.

I also remembered Tim and me praying specifically that, in spite of our weakness, God would somehow receive glory to Himself through this situation and through our lives. And it blows me away that God honored that prayer, and even in spite of our pitiful humanity, Christ who was living in us by faith, was being demonstrated even when we were unaware of it. Somehow His life was shining through our tattered veil of flesh.

GOD GETS THE GLORY

Maybe you have thought that God's glory is only revealed through magnificent super saints who are doing extraordinary things, people who "have it all together," and whose lives seem to run in seamless perfection. Oswald Chambers said, "Spirituality is not divorced from the sordid realities of life." Even Jesus dealt in the ordinary, sordid and inglorious things! Things like basins, towels, sandals, and dirty feet, impatient crowds, hypocrites, taxes, sleeplessness, exhaustion, and the sharing of daily life with twelve sometimes stubborn and irritating disciples. And we mustn't forget the pain and humiliation of the beatings, crown of thorns and the cross. Everything that He did and endured on this earth was so that His Father in Heaven might be glorified.

And so I realized that as we believed, even in the drudgery, exhaustion and terrifying reality of those days, the glory of God was being revealed, and His power was truly being made perfect in our weakness.

Tim and I will never seek to understand all the reasons that Jesse was stricken with cancer and rendered blind. We will not try to validate things which we cannot validate. Our limited human perspective has made it impossible to find explanations which satisfy all the questions. I will honestly admit that we have felt ourselves revolting at times against high and lofty "answers" from people who haven't been where we've been. Through grace, though, we have chosen to turn our eyes to our awesome loving Father who continues to turn such bitter events into so much good for us and into so much glory for Himself. We have witnessed some of this glory in the encouragement hurting people have received as we have shared bits and pieces of our story with those He has placed within our scope of influence.

After returning to the Philippines, Tim was approached by one of our pastors who lives deep in the mountains of one of the mountain provinces. While yet in his early twenties, this godly now middle-aged man was wonderfully saved from a life of wickedness and vice and subsequently called into the ministry. Pastor Guibong has become a humble servant and an influential church leader who has led many to Christ. He and his faithful wife Susan, even while quite poor by Western standards, are busy parents of seven children, one of whom is severely handicapped. This young girl spends almost every waking hour sitting in a chair lovingly made by her father from wood he cut in a nearby forest. She doesn't speak nor seem to hear or understand anything that is happening around her, and she is completely dependent upon her parents for every aspect of life.

Pastor Francis Guibong and Tim stood on the lawn outside our home on a warm summer evening and talked about the lessons God had taught each of them through the pain of sick and suffering children. Francis testified that the grace he had witnessed as we had walked through our appointed valley had encouraged him to continue trusting the Lord as he walked through the valley God had appointed for him. He became quite emotional as he shared how God had used his daughter's illness to purify his heart, to bring him to a place of complete surrender to God's wisdom. He talked of how he had asked God over and over again for a miracle and how for some years he had struggled with anger over his daughter's condition. Pastor Francis admitted that he had chafed for a time at his daughter's sickness not only for her sake but also for his. Her suffering had brought such a hardship upon their struggling family, and he had not understood why God would call him into full-time ministry and not remove this painful thorn of suffering. God's placement of a severely disabled child in such a remote, rustic environment not only seemed cruel but also a hindrance to real ministry. Tim recalls that some of Pastor Guibong's reasoning had gone something like this:

- Couldn't I do much more for God if only God would heal my child?

- Wouldn't God get so much more glory by healing her?

- How can I preach God's power effectively if my own prayers go unanswered?

But Pastor Francis went on to explain the victory God worked in his heart. One night in utter brokenness and desperation he wept out a prayer of complete surrender, "Lord, I can't carry this burden and anger anymore! I yield to your will and to your wisdom! I surrender myself and my suffering child and our ministry to you!" He testified that as he surrendered himself to whatever would bring God most glory that night his daughter ceased being a burden and became a blessing instead! A flood of divine peace and joy washed through his heart, and he sensed God's deep purifying grace. And he testified that from that moment he began to understand that God had ordained this trial—this weakness in his life—to humble him, sanctify him and to keep him completely dependent upon Himself.

Shortly after we returned to the United States in 2009, Jesse was invited to play a piano piece in the annual Piano Extravaganza concert in Shipshewana Indiana, a program my sister, Kim Collingsworth, was hosting. Jesse loves the piano and has played since he was about five years old, and even though he had only a small part in the program it was an amazing opportunity for him. There were approximately fifteen hundred people in the crowd the first night as he played. Before he came on stage Kim introduced him by telling a small part of his story. She included the fact that he had spent most of his life living in the Philippines where his parents were missionaries.

Not long after the concert I received a letter from a woman who had been in the auditorium that night. She had heard Jesse play and wanted to share with me what had taken place in her own life. She and her husband had been called to be missionaries in the country of Haiti. While there she had given birth to a child, and when he was very young it was discovered that he was deaf. "We were devastated!" she said. She went on to share that they made the decision, based upon what they felt his needs would be, to abandon their missionary work and bring the child back to the States.

Two or three years later, however, this missionary couple began to get a strong sense that God was calling them to return to Haiti—a calling they resisted. She related, "We were thinking, 'Look, there's just no way that we can raise a deaf child in the third world.'" But the more they resisted the stronger the calling came. They simply could not get away from this seemingly impossible calling of God. This dear woman shared with me that she had begun asking the Lord to verify this call by bringing another family into their lives—one who had successfully raised a child with a handicap on the mission field. This mother was in the crowd on that night as Kim told Jesse's story. She shared with me that she had sat there weeping as she listened to Jesse—who was blind and had been raised on the mission field—play the piano on that night. She knew that God had answered her prayer!

I was astounded that God had brought this woman, (who was from another state and only visiting family in the area) to that piano concert and that Jesse just "happened" to be there. I could clearly see that it was in direct answer to this one mother's prayer that Jesse had received the invitation to play. God is so big, and so wise, and so sovereign. And He was glorified on that night!

As His people trust Him, God always turns curses into blessings. I am reminded of the story in the Bible of Balaam. He was hired by the Moabites to curse God's people. Scripture tells us, however, that God turned the plan of Satan on its head and turned the curse into a blessing. The most powerful part of this drama for me, however, is the reason the Bible gives for this turn. Moses encouraged Israel by telling them that an intended curse became a blessing, *"Because the LORD your God loves you"* (Deuteronomy 23:5). It was because of God's love for His people that He completely over-turned the evil intention of the enemy.

We live in a sin-cursed world and one where suffering abounds for all of us! Satan is constantly roaming about, *"seeking whom he may devour"* (I Peter 5:8). But for the believer, his absolute worst does not have the power to destroy us. I am convinced that there is not a circumstance in your life or mine that God doesn't wish, out of His great love for us, to turn into a blessing. And when we submit to Him, resisting the natural desire that demands for God to immediately extricate us from our situation, it is then we can sit back in wonder as He pours out His grace upon us. We are blessed and He is glorified!

CHAPTER TEN

—◦◦◦—

The Rest of the Story

*What if I have eyes that do not see
This gaily colored world of forms and show:
What if in the dark I always go,
My footsteps led by sounds and memory:
What if the sunset always hides its glow,
And morning's dawn does not unveil to me:
My father gave me strength of soul and mind:
My mother taught me how to laugh and pray:
My ears and nose and fingers are designed
To bring me knowledge, beauty, work, and play–
I do not envy those who see the light,
For I know my way and have no fear of night.
Faith means believing what is incredible,
or it is no virtue at all.
Hope means hoping when things are hopeless,
or it is no virtue at all.
And charity means pardoning what is unpardonable,
or it is no virtue at all.*
G. K. Chesterton

EYES TO SEE

JUST RECENTLY, WHILE GOING THROUGH SOME OLD PICTURES, I came across a photo of Jesse taken shortly after he became blind. In it he was standing in the middle of our kitchen. A brilliant shaft of morning sun was casting its gleam across the floor in front of him. He stood there holding the tiniest white, red-tipped cane. He was leaning forward almost resting his chin on the end of the cane. As I stared at this picture and the pensive look on his small face, my eyes filled with tears, and I swallowed several times to remove the lump that rose in my throat. It took me back to the moment that I had snapped that picture and the enormity of what he was feeling then and what we all were experiencing in those early days. It seemed impossible to even imagine a bright future for him.

He was adamantly against the use of that cane and told me very insistently, "Canes are for old people!" He was bewildered and confused at our insistence that he carry that thing around. One day I told him that it would enable him to go places and be independent as an adult, but his reply shocked me: "I'm not going to be blind when I grow up." There was no anger. It was just a four-year-old's inability to fully comprehend the long term nature of things.

The look on his face in that one picture captured what we were all feeling. It was as if everything in our lives had been tossed up into the air, and uncertainty seemed to abound in all our hearts. We were certain about the God that we served; we believed that He had a plan and was leading, but the details of life and our future seemed to be wavering on a sea of variables that we could no longer control.

Both Tim and I greatly desired to return to the Philippines and to the people that we had been called to serve. However, each of us entertained the thought that perhaps Jesse's blindness had closed that door. I would argue repeatedly, "Tim, God gave us brains, and smart people do not take a blind child to a third world country where resources are limited." Although our involvement in missions hadn't waned and Tim had made at least twelve trips to the Philippines during the four years of Jesse's illness, I felt that surely God had another plan in mind for us now. Surely He wanted us to do what was best for Jesse, and in my mind staying in the USA, where privileges and opportunities for blind people abound, was best. I will forever be grateful for a husband who is patient and loving and didn't "un-spiritualize" me or invalidate my questions and fears.

In early November we were offered a very attractive ministry position at a church in another state. Our mission's leadership knew that we were in the valley of decision and stood behind us as we worked our way through it. We'll always be grateful for their love and patience. Tim met with the church board, and we began praying about the invitation. It made sense. It was challenging. It fit our gifts. It would put us in close proximity to excellent resources for Jesse and a reputable children's hospital. It would allow us to work with some wonderful people. For some reason we didn't have perfect peace about it, and yet we couldn't think of any reason to turn down the invitation. We thought that perhaps this lack of peace was just a fear of change. Surely this move was the right one! After a lengthy conversation one morning, we decided together that by evening, unless the Lord gave clear guidance otherwise, Tim would call the leadership of the church and accept the position.

Late that evening after putting the kids to bed, I was tidying the house, in an attempt to pick up the pieces of a busy day, when Tim walked into the kitchen. "Becky," He said with a tone in his voice that made me stop what I was doing and look up, "I know without a doubt what it is that God wants for us to do." He continued, "The Lord has just answered our prayer and opened my eyes to His will. We are going to return to the Philippines!" I was shocked at his words, but even more surprised at the absolute peace that flowed through my heart and mind. I knew in that moment that He was right, and have not doubted it since. Once again the Lord opened the door just in the nick of time!

It may seem to some that we were weak to doubt God's calling or to even consider that maybe we should deviate from our original plan to return to the Philippines. After all, God had so clearly and miraculously led us to this point. Maybe we were slow to really believe, but this only proves to me the power of God. We wanted nothing more than to fulfill God's perfect plan. We also wanted to be good parents and to obey in the area of caring for the needs of our family. God knew our hearts, and I realize now, even more than I did then, that when we truly are seeking His will and hold loosely to our own wisdom and reasoning, He will never let us "accidentally" miss His divine purpose for our lives.

Three short months later I found myself sitting on an airplane with my husband, three children and a newly acquired, four-month-old, golden retriever named "Buddy." I sat there not with foresight and knowledge as to how God was going to work out the details but rather with total assurance that this was exactly what God's plan was for our family. But this assurance did not necessarily block the temptations that would come.

I heard the pilot's voice announcing that we were beginning our descent into Manila and would be on the ground in about thirty minutes. I was totally unprepared for the mental onslaught of the enemy that overwhelmed me in the final moments of that flight. Satan began screaming into my thoughts that this was ludicrous! My heart was gripped with the fear that this was not going to work out! Jesse would not have his needs met educationally; perhaps his cancer would come back, and Satan specifically said to me, "You just wait; within a few months you'll be sitting on a plane just like this one heading back home in utter defeat!" I felt physically sick!

THE REST OF THE STORY

All was quiet around me; the children were sacked out—exhausted from this twenty-four hour trip, and so I reached for my Bible. I opened it up and began reading the words of the prophet Jeremiah. I came to Jeremiah 24:6 and read these beautiful words. *"For I will set mine eyes upon them for good, and I will bring them again to this Land, and I will build them and not pull them down: and I will plant them and not pluck them up"* (KJV). Peace flowed into my troubled mind and with it the knowledge that God was speaking to me through His Word. I knew that God was directly refuting the attack of Satan and reaffirming His promise and calling on our lives.

And so we began life again living in a foreign country, far from home and all that was familiar. I was absolutely delighted with the new house that had been built during our time in the US. It was beautiful in every way and most importantly, according to our builder, "Rat proofed!" We were warmly welcomed by our Filipino brothers and sisters and our co-workers, David and Christina Black and their children, Robert and Roanna.

I immediately noticed that there was one room in the house that was full of what appeared to be boxes of junk. One afternoon I began to open boxes and was amazed to find all our belongings that had been left behind four years earlier. Honestly, I hadn't even given these things a second thought until now. Helen Forto, the wife of our college president, had rescued them from the old house before it had been destroyed. As I began sifting through the boxes, waves of nostalgia washed over me. I found bags of newborn diapers and beautiful baby clothes with the tags still on—these were to have been Jesse's but he never wore them. I held a tiny pair of blue flip flops in my hands and remembered our three-year-old "Timmers" sporting these around the campus. He had been a toddler then and was now a big boy of seven. The room was like a time capsule that encased so many things from our life before. It seemed a lifetime ago that we had hurriedly packed a couple of suitcases for our "four weeks" in the States. I was overwhelmed by God's goodness in carrying us through what had actually become four years of struggle, tears, uncertainty and an abundance of grace. We had come full circle! I could hardly believe that we were here.

The children were happy. Valerie at eleven was thrilled to have Roanna Black as an instant best friend, and the two were inseparable. Timothy began making many friends immediately and especially loved playing guitar with the Bible College Students. Jesse quickly learned the layout of the campus and navigated around very independently. He talked with everyone he met and became an instant object of affection and also curiosity to all who lived on the campus, and even the surrounding community.

One day, shortly after we had arrived, I heard drilling and someone banging about on our front porch. I went to investigate and found our friend and builder, Bro. Zaldy, installing a doorbell. I knew that we hadn't ordered a doorbell, but he quickly told me that Jesse had come to him and told him that he wanted a "ding dong" on our front porch! Bro. Zaldy obliged and so we got a doorbell. We laughed about it but scolded Jesse for taking matters into his own hands. We also informed Bro. Zaldy that he really didn't have to do the bidding of a four year old!

We did find this deference to Jesse to be a bit of a problem. We often had Bible College students working in our house (this helped them to pay their school bills), and very often Timothy and Valerie took the brunt of things. On one occasion, Jesse wanted a toy that Timothy had, and when Timothy wouldn't give it, our Filipino helper scolded him saying, "Timmers, let him have it, he's blind!" Well, this didn't fly well with the older kids at all! I had to step in and let people know on more than one occasion that Jesse couldn't have everything he wanted just because of his blindness. "Children who are treated like this," I explained, "end up in prison!"

THE REST OF THE STORY

I was anxious to begin Jesse's training and will forever be grateful for our friends Bob and Kay Bickert and Paul and Jan Turner. They are veteran missionaries who then taught at the Wesleyan college in a town about fifteen minutes from ours. They had become dear friends and mentors to us during our first year in the Philippines. Bob mentioned that they had several blind students at their college and a teacher who came from Manila to help with the adaptation and brailing for these blind young people. He said that although she had never worked with a small child, she was willing to try teaching Jesse.

Mylen worked for an organization called "Resources for the Blind," and was based out of Manila. This ministry was, and still is, headed up by wonderful missionaries, Randy and Marla Weissart. They are natives of Alaska but, by that time, had already spent twenty plus years as missionaries in the Philippines. In addition to being passionate about helping the blind, they are the parents of thirteen children. They were so kind and generous and thrilled at the prospect of their employee being able to help a blind missionary kid.

Tim and I were overjoyed and amazed at how God had obviously made a way for us. We lived five hours from Manila, and it was unbelievable that there just happened to be a teacher for the blind who was stationed only fifteen minutes from our home. This, in a country where most blind people never have the opportunity to learn, and their best hope is to be able to eek out a living either begging or giving back massages in the market.

I well remember our first meeting with "Ate Mye." (Ate means "big sister, and this is what she wanted Jesse to call her.) She was young, in her late twenties, very short, maybe five feet tall and tiny. She walked with a cane, and I noticed that one foot was deformed. I felt a bit of concern as I tried to imagine how this frail looking girl could possibly handle our very strong-willed and newly blind four year old. We introduced ourselves and Jesse and decided that we would come each Monday and Thursday afternoon for one hour sessions. She would begin with the basics of Braille. The lessons would take place in the house where she stayed on the campus of the Wesleyan Bible College. It was a wooden structure, very hot inside, and rather dilapidated.

On the first day of Jesse's lessons, Ate Mye informed Jesse that his first lesson would be to navigate using his cane from my car to the front door of her house. This was a distance of about one hundred feet, and she wanted him to do it … alone! I followed behind, a little nervous as Jesse tapped along the sidewalk towards the direction of her voice. She stood waiting on her front porch and would call out to him from time to time. Halfway there he became totally frustrated, threw the cane to the ground and stated vehemently, "I'm not doing this!" I rushed to his side and bent to pick up the cane only to hear Ate Mye say firmly, "No, Becky, do not pick it up, Jesse will retrieve his own cane." I stopped, slowly straightened up and backed away. After all, I was the mom; my son had only been blind for four months, and I was clueless as to how to handle situations like this. Jesse realized that I wasn't going to rescue him, and I watched helplessly as he felt around on the ground, found the cane, picked it up and made his way to the front porch. I left that day feeling much more certain that Ate Mye could indeed handle herself—and Jesse—just fine!

Jesse struggled in the beginning and spent his second lesson sitting on my lap. He wasn't happy with the set-up at all. When we arrived for the third time, Ate Mye sat Jesse in his chair and told him that they would begin each lesson with prayer. She explained to him that she would ask God to help her to be able to teach him. I can see them even now, Jesse—his small curly head bent over the Perkins Brailler on the table in front of him and Mye, leaning on her cane, head bowed, asking God for His help.

This was the beginning of a deep and trusting relationship between the two of them. She was indeed a gift to our family and especially to Jesse. She spent the next nearly eight years training him and laying the foundation for learning that would enable him to excel in school. He learned to read and write Braille and to work complicated math problems using the Cranmer abacus. He learned to navigate using a white cane, and so much more. Ate Mye adapted our Scrabble game, brailing the tiles, and they played Scrabble and Uno for hours.

The beautiful thing about Ate Mye was that, unlike many Filipinos, she didn't pity Jesse. I learned that her father and also several of her uncles were blind. Her father had worked at a myriad of jobs to provide for the needs of his wife and six children. Mye told us with pride that he had never begged for even one peso but had earned his way. He had insisted that his children go to school and work hard. It was evident that his persistence had been passed on to them. Mye was stricken with polio as a small child and left crippled, but she never let it stop her.

It was Ate Mye who, to my horror, first broke the news to Jesse that he was handicapped. One day I was driving Jesse home from Mye's house after a Braille lesson. I was quiet and totally focused on the narrow crowded streets where bicycles, tricycles (motor bikes with side cars) animals and people were everywhere. I had only recently begun driving in the Philippines, and both hands were gripping the steering wheel as I slowly navigated the busy streets. Jesse suddenly piped up with a startling question. "Mom, am I handicapped?" He went on, "Ate Mye told me today that I'm handicapped." I momentarily forgot about the crazy traffic and my nervousness about driving. I thought, "What a foolish thing for her to do! How in the world do I answer a question like this?" I regained some composure and thought about how I could answer this delicately and without damaging his tender emotions. A few moments later, and after my long and pitiful monologue about what it really means to be handicapped versus just inconvenienced by blindness, he said in an exasperated tone of voice, "So does that mean that when I grow up, I'm gonna have to park my car in one of those handicapped parking places?" I couldn't believe it! That was all that he was concerned about. I decided right then to leave the "You're never going to drive" conversation for another day!

As we walked daily by faith and trusting in our wonderful God, we began to see, with eyes wide open, God's perfect plan unfold. We were amazed as we watched Him, one by one, uncover and lay to rest the lies of Satan. These lies had, from time to time, despite our daily choice to trust, nagged at our consciousness from that very first day in a Grand Rapids doctor's office. Lies that said this was the end for us and for Jesse; that we couldn't make it; that God wouldn't provide; that this trial would destroy us; that ministry in the Philippines was impossible. These and a host of others dissipated before the powerful, unshakable promises of God.

Indeed, as we've watched our son grow, and learn, and thrive we've become keenly aware of the fact that the God we serve is truly the God of the rest of the story. Our story and Jesse's has been written on His heart from the beginning of time and is playing out each day just as He ordained and designed it to. We realize not only that cancer or blindness cannot thwart His plan but that they are actually interwoven creatively and lovingly into that beautiful plan.

And the story continues—it is still being written. God's work of grace amazes us daily. Jesse is now a bright and well-adjusted 15 year old. Are there struggles? Of course there are many! Blindness is no walk in the park, nor is it something that we would have chosen for him. He most certainly would not have chosen it. We are sometimes painfully aware of the many things that he must conquer and learn in order to live a full and independent life. We sometimes grieve over things he misses out on that other kids enjoy. But I remember reading in the Scriptures, *"And I will give thee treasures of darkness and hidden riches of secret places"* (Isaiah 45:3).

Treasures of darkness? Hidden riches? I began to see them years ago as I watched Jesse at the age of seven hike fearlessly in the rainforest of the Philippines while hanging onto his dad's backpack for guidance, listened to him read his very first book in braille, watched him and Timothy swim with joyful abandon in the South China Sea, and watched as he handed out candy and vitamins to poor village children during medical missions. More recently, I've trembled with equal amounts of delight and trepidation as he skimmed across the shimmering water of Smith Mountain Lake in Virginia on a pair of water skis, (his dad, brother and cousins wildly cheering him on!), and sometimes these days I simply close my eyes and bask in the sound of him playing "Great is Thy Faithfulness" on the piano. These have been treasures of darkness, treasures only a good, loving and wise God would give! These moments, and so many others, have been gifts from our heavenly Father so lovingly scattered like tiny nuggets of gold on a shadowy pathway, their beauty and brightness gleaming at some of the most unexpected moments.

Pastor Erwin Lutzer recently said in a sermon preached from the life of Job, "The purpose in suffering is not so that we will know the deep purposes of God but that we will know God." In the story of our lives we don't need to know how tomorrow's page will read but only the One who is writing the script. Do you know Him? Do you know Him as Father? Do you know Him as Lord? Does He have permission to do as He sees best in your life and in the life of your family? Are you daily surrendering your all to Him?

EYES TO SEE

If you are a child of God then you, too, can rest assured that He is authoring every line in the story of your life. He knows the pain and suffering which fills that page in the chapter you are currently living. He understands your desire to flip back to the pages of a happier time or to move ahead quickly and even skip this painful chapter altogether. (Did not Jesus also cry out for His Father to remove the bitter cup He was about to drink?) To run from your sufferings, however, will cause you to miss the great comfort and peace God wants to give you, and the contentment and character He longs to produce in you, right now! Right where you are. Through your suffering, God will reveal life-transforming glimpses of Himself which you will never enjoy except through pain. He's washing your eyes with tears that you might see more clearly! You may be weeping now, but joy awaits you in the morning! And know this: Out of the same pen that is writing your story flows not only wisdom for the writing, but rivers of grace for the living. Will you dare to believe?

Musical artists Ben Glover and Josh Wilson have written a powerful song which challenges us toward joyful expectation even when everything we see and feel screams that we've been forsaken,

> *Would you dare, would you dare to believe*
> *That you still have a reason to sing?*
> *Cause the pain that you've been feeling*
> *It can't compare to the joy that's coming!*
>
> *So hold on, you've got to wait for the light.*
> *Press on and just fight the good fight.*
> *Cause the pain that you've been feeling,*
> *It's just the dark before the morning!*

Some may think it a strange thing for a parent to say to his child, but Tim has sometimes reminded Jesse, "Son, you've got to make it to heaven because if, for love of this world or the love of momentary, sinful pleasures you should turn from the God who sent His Son to redeem you, then you will never … never see again—not in this life, not in eternity! But, Jesse, if you will put your faith and hope in Jesus, and if you will, by His grace, live for His glory in this life, then blindness for you is only a momentary affliction. And the next face you'll see will be the face of Jesus!"

"For our light affliction, which is but for a moment,
is working for us a far more exceeding and eternal weight of glory,
while we do not look at the things which are seen,
but at the things which are not seen.
For the things which are seen are temporary,
but the things which are not seen are eternal."
2 Cor. 4:17-18

EVERYONE HAS A STORY TO TELL!

Becky and Tim would love for you to share yours on the Eyes To See Facebook page!

 Eyes2SeeBook